SM98005407
7/99.
£15.95.
JJO T
(Tay)

Redcoats and Patriots

Reflective Practice in Drama and Social Studies

Philip Taylor

√

HEINEMANN
Portsmouth, NH

Heinemann
A division of Reed Elsevier Inc.
361 Hanover Street
Portsmouth, NH 03801–3912
http://www.heinemann.com

Offices and agents throughout the world

No identifiers of the students or school are given in this book. However, I have endeavored to keep intact the students' original writing and utterances, including their own expressions, spelling, and grammar.

Library of Congress Cataloging-in-Publication Data
Taylor, Philip.
    Redcoats and patriots : reflective practice in drama and social
studies / Philip Taylor.
        p.   cm.
    Includes bibliographical references.
    ISBN 0–325–00028–X (alk. paper)
    1. Drama in education.   2. Social studies—Study and teaching.
I. Title.
PN3171.T39   1998
373.139'9—DC21   98–18984
                                                                            CIP

Editor: Lisa A. Barnett
Production: Vicki Kasabian
Cover design: Jenny Jensen Greenleaf
Author photograph: Paula Court
Manufacturing: Courtney Ordway

Printed in the United States of America on acid-free paper
02 01 00 99 98 ML 1 2 3 4 5

Contents

Foreword by Cecily O'Neill   v

Preface   ix

Introduction: Understanding Context and Taking Charge   1

1   Process Drama and Cultural Capital   14

2   Understanding from Within:
Learning in Process Drama   44

3   Shifting Perspectives:
Learning Through Process Drama   60

4   Building a Knowledge Base:
Learning About Process Drama   109

5   Reflective-Practitioner Research   125

6   The Future   144

Resource List: Books on Process Drama   161

Bibliography   167

Foreword

Teachers are created by their encounters with their students. *Redcoats and Patriots* is an absorbing and highly personal account of a teacher changing and being changed by his students. Philip Taylor's classroom encounters transform his attitudes to his students, his beliefs about education, and his understanding of the potential of process drama.

Meanings generated in the classroom are shaped by the lived context of both teacher and students. Each of them is bound by his or her own cultural perspective and experience. All of Philip Taylor's efforts to enrich his curriculum occur within a recognizable educational environment and one that is not always sympathetic to his purposes. His view of learning as essentially collaborative and negotiated seems out of place in an institution dominated by a conservative transmission model of education. His realistic understanding of traditional curriculum expectations and timetable constraints will reassure other teachers hoping to move beyond these limits to a more open and genuinely dialogic classroom experience.

These limitations were overcome by the discovery of teacher-based action research and the notion of the reflective practitioner. Philip Taylor reflects honestly on his own failures of technique and understanding and learns from the sometimes surprisingly powerful insights of his students. As he develops as a critical theorist, he gives his students the opportunity to build their own powers of questioning and reflect on their own learning. As he puts it, when teachers begin to ask questions about their purposes they are acting in a professional manner. But when they ask whose interests are being served by the study of particular material, what values are being reinforced, and what students are expected to do with this knowledge, they are asking questions within a critical framework.

Philip Taylor has been much influenced by the pioneering work of Dorothy Heathcote and Gavin Bolton. Heathcote insists that in devising fruitful encounters between teacher, students, ideas, knowledge, and skills, it is essential to become process-oriented. If we are to become authentic teachers we must:

- learn to present problems differently to students
- discover more subtle forms of induction and communication
- encourage student interaction and decision making
- imagine and carry into action a greater variety of tasks
- develop a range of feedback techniques
- take risks with materials
- tolerate ambiguity
- pay attention to detail.

As the students explore the relationship between Redcoats and Patriots in this social studies classroom, each of these essential elements comes into play. Throughout, the teacher alters his plans and adjusts his questioning to accommodate students' interests, understanding, and responses. Working in a highly cognitive and collaborative way, the students:

- take on roles as historians of the future, citizens of Boston, British soldiers, and patriots
- decipher and interpret authentic materials
- narrate and reconstruct historical incidents
- create scenes and tableaux
- carry out research on characters and topics of their choice
- write reports, journals, letters
- speculate, solve problems, make decisions
- reflect on their own and others' work
- make connections between their discoveries in drama and their real lives.

The students, as they undertake these varied and challenging tasks, achieve an impressive level of engagement. This engagement is active, not just in a physical sense, but in the making of meaning. It is creative, as they step inside the imagined world of eighteenth-century Boston and bring to life its people and events. It is collaborative, and includes the intellectual, emotional, and imaginative contributions of everyone in the class, including the teacher. These collective responses do not submerge the identity of the students. Instead, the participants experience their own inner dramas and express them in their writing and responses.

Because drama is essentially a social and inclusive art, it creates a sense of community. The students are all involved in the same enterprise as they struggle to make sense of their experience and emerging knowledge. Because the people and events of the drama are placed in a historical context, students create and experience a community struggling for social and political change. The students are not merely observers of this struggle but participants in it. The drama provides a world of possibilities and invites them to take action in it. They begin to think of themselves as people who can make things happen, who can work together in situations fraught with danger, and who can strive together for justice and equality. As Herbert Kohl (1995) puts it,

> Without the encouragement of the social imagination, of freedom to imagine the world being other than it is, we are left without hope for society as a whole. (62–63)

Imaginative engagement at this level is not a precise or disciplined affair. It may be regarded as disorder by colleagues and administrators, but this apparent confusion is often evidence that students are participating and is a sign of social inclusiveness.

Drama has the power to involve us, to touch our imaginations, and to enlarge our sense of self. Throughout this book, Philip Taylor never forgets that he is working in the art form of drama. This realization underpins all his questioning, structuring, and planning. He recognizes that drama is never just a way of making a statement or delivering information, but an energizing experience and a source of insight. Whether on the stage or in the classroom, it consists of a series of interactions of increasing intensity. This book progresses in a similar manner as the students begin to accept the parameters of the imagined world they have been invited to inhabit and explore the range of their freedoms within that world. These freedoms build a new relationship with their teacher as they make their voices heard in the classroom and break free from the narrow social roles that constrain them. The collective nature of their drama experience in the social studies classroom strengthens their personal security and affirms their existence.

Teachers of all subjects will be refreshed and inspired by this honest account of students in a familiar school setting, who reach new levels of competence and understanding through their experience of process drama in the social studies classroom.

Cecily O'Neill

Preface

The first Friday of each month always created great joy for the children; regular afternoon classes were canceled so that the faculty could meet. One such day, as the children prepared to leave early, I secretly hoped the principal would not exceed the meeting's scheduled finishing time of 2:00 P.M. It was Friday, after all, and I needed the full weekend to contemplate the drama lesson I had taught that day.

As I entered the meeting room, laden with kids' journals and my own logbook, I noticed the grim look on the other teachers' faces. I recalled how prior to this meeting rumors had been circulating that budgetary limitations would influence drastically the school's operations for the next year. We all knew that severe cuts were coming. The written agenda that the principal had circulated indicated that there was much material to discuss, including grant writing, the current financial status, plans for the next year, the projected income, the children's study habits, a proposal for more fund-raising drives, and summer school arrangements.

These concerns seemed far away to me, especially as I noticed Meryl's journal piece, which she had written in role as an eighteenth-century American patriot. "I couldn't act suspicious and I couldn't accuse him or approach him," she had written in response to an antagonistic part I had enacted, "I had to find out more about him." How was it possible, I wondered, for her role work and writing to carry such conviction in our drama, when her other teachers said she was passive and docile in class?

We were meeting in one of the classrooms, and the faculty were sitting in the children's desks, those ancient wooden "rat traps" with the inkwell at the apex. I continued to muse over the students' responses in the drama. Meryl's seventh-grade classroom had been

ix

transformed into an eighteenth-century Bostonian tavern and Meryl, unbelievably, was at its center. On this day, we had been exploring in social studies the Boston Massacre, an event from American Revolutionary history in which the Boston patriots under the leadership of William Molineux and Sam Adams were planning tactics to overcome the growing presence of the redcoats—the British soldiers—or "lobsterbacks" (as they were referred to by the Sons of Liberty, a radical group that worked for American independence).

The Massacre, a propaganda term designed by Adams, refers to the shooting of a number of colonists by the British soldiers. My aim was to have the students commit to the patriot cause and consider the contradictory pressures posed by this cause, pressures related to nationhood and identity. Enacting a gathering of eighteenth-century patriots who would canvass strategies for curbing the growing British presence might usefully help us explore these pressures further. The students presumed that I would act the role of their leader, Molineux, during the meeting. However, as a tension-generating device before the drama, I informed the kids that Molineux was delayed and that they, in role as the patriots, would be greeted by an unknown figure.

As the drama unfolded, and as I became more duplicitous as this shady character, Meryl and her fellow "patriots" became more threatening. "What is your oath?" she challenged me as I muttered an excuse for Molineux's absence. "What's the password?" she persisted. As I became more elusive, she became more decisive, at one point even uniting all her fellow patriots-students against me, persuading them that I was enacting a British spy. How was it that this particular drama on this day transformed Meryl into an assertive and commanding leader?

All sixteen teachers of this inner-city school were now present, and I was thrown back to reality as the principal, an Irish American nun in her early forties, entered. She was into her second year as principal of the school and treated her position with vigor and commitment. She had appointed me as an eighth-grade homeroom teacher with a further responsibility for teaching social studies to the seventh grade. I think she was becoming quite suspicious of my drama work and was questioning, in her own mind, how drama related to the curriculum guidelines, which had been recommended by her superiors. She had commented on the unconventional nature of the work—the fact that the students were out of their desks, acting out roles in a variety of different groupings. On a few occasions she had asked, What did all this drama have to do with social studies? What was the nature of the learning going on? Why were they making noise? Now I temporarily put my student journals aside and forced myself to give her my complete attention.

"You're laying excellent foundations for our *350* children," she began to address us in her melodically powerful brogue while positioning herself and her papers in the confined space of the desk. "You're not letting up on them," she exhorted. "The children are heavily supervised during the day; in the *yard* at lunchtime teachers are constantly present. Things are not let go." My mind started to wander while she preceded to list the numerous ways the children were "heavily supervised." Why was it that she always referred to the *350* children and the enforced manner in which they were controlled in the yard? Yard! At this school one quickly learned that *yard* was a reference to the daily fifteen-minute recess, taken literally in an open space on the roof of the school. Recreation space was at a premium in this environment. How I dreaded this supervision, particularly trying to enforce the no-running or no-ball-playing rule. I believed that supervising children's playtime was difficult for teachers at the best of times, but it was nearly impossible with children who were not allowed to do the usual play activities such as running, ball kicking, and other physical exertions at lunch recess.

Boston, Boston. I fidgeted with my papers and recalled that Albert had commented to me once that in social studies he had been conditioned to answer teachers' questions and not engage in conversations with them. He never challenged the teachers' authority, even when he disagreed with them. It appeared that these dividing lines between teachers and students had been drilled into both parties from the early years.

The school, the principal was reminding the teachers, was in an area of the city where crime was "an ever present threat." The previous week a parent had been shot in a nearby side street. A Mafia connection was assumed. She continued, "The children feel *safe* here, and that's one of the reasons why the parents send them to this school." Safety *was* a major issue, but with all of the physical controls placed on the 350 children, I wondered how emotionally safe they were. Is the control over students' minds a safety mechanism as well? I thought of Meryl and Albert and wondered what kind of education their parents hoped they would receive in the school. Would drama be seen as a diversion from regular curriculum activity? How might parents used to conventional approaches toward learning and the social studies curriculum react when they discovered that the children were imagining that they were Boston patriots planning tactics to curb the increasing presence of the British soldiers? In my view, these kids were released from the constraints of their own personalities in drama, and were challenged to decide on seeming matters of life and death. Would parents be surprised or encouraged by their children's posturing?

As the principal continued recalling the perils of the school's location, I quietly agreed that she was not exaggerating about the area. Walking both to and from the school, I often had to negotiate a cautious path through the garbage-strewn streets with their homeless people and drug pushers. I remembered how my first memories of the neighborhood focused on the pungent smell of human excrement, and on the gangs of youth harboring on street corners. Was it only ten years ago that I was teaching theatre in an Australian middle-class high school? Who would have thought that within a decade I would be teaching seventh grade in what a colleague described once as an inner-city American ghetto?

But for all the violence in the community, I was continually struck by the sense of harmony, collaboration, and collegiality that my seventh graders would comment on when they experienced drama. "I remember when I saw this older child, Albert," Tom would write in his journal, "always argueing with this other boy, me, in the 1st couple of weeks." The drama work would change all of that. "In the last days I see them working together and sharing our ideas." Amara, too, described how "more comfortable and relaxed" she felt. She reflected on the group's ability to "not argue with their classmates."

My mind slowly refocused on the sharp and penetrating tones of the principal's dialect. Despite the odds of poverty, she was saying, the pervasiveness of single-parent families, the frequent reports of child abuse, and the lack of community interest in the school, she firmly believed that the children received "a very good education." Perhaps if she were in my social studies classroom today, I thought, she might retract those words. Drama activity in this school, I surmised, was often seen to be in contradiction to "a very good education."

Most of her days, she now proceeded to explain, were spent in administrative meetings with the district office, or having consultations with accountants and discussions with other principals. Her mathematical background was the only saving grace in coping with the huge financial debt of the school. "I think we can make it, though," she said while scanning what appeared to be a balance sheet, "if certain procedures are followed in the forthcoming year."

She spoke to us as if we were her submissive students, and I wondered if perhaps this was one reason why she scheduled faculty meetings in classrooms with the teachers oddly seated in children's desks. "Five teaching positions have to be terminated at the end of the year," she calmly said. What was that? Each teacher's head seemed to crank up an inch or two. "I suspect there will be natural attrition here, so *let's not* dwell on it." Funny how we were encouraged not to dwell on matters that focused on our ongoing livelihood.

"Money-making efforts must become more a part of the cultural life of the school," she quickly continued, seemingly changing track and possibly suspecting that I was going to ask a difficult question. Funny, I thought, that cultural life in this parochial school was now tied into money making. The teachers would be expected to take an active role in all of these finance-raising efforts. Even then she was not certain that the school would be able to remain solvent. However, the fears of having to close down were being subordinated for now. Close down? Where did this option come from? Should I ask?

Before I could formulate my cloudy thoughts into a question, she moved on to another topic. Class sizes would have to be dramatically increased in the next year; some teachers would have forty students in their room. Forty students doing drama, I sighed. Was this measure a conspiracy against the arts? Such constraints, she asserted, meant that severe economical measures would be faced. Teachers, among other things, were requested to keep future orders of textbooks and stationery to an absolute minimum. I was anxious to get away from her demands and to return to my reflections on the drama.

"I don't want to trust him," wrote Albert about the role I had assumed in our work today, "which would make the story very much more exciting." And then there was Tom's reflection on the power of drama: "When we're working as a group we don't feel lonely or having to face the neglections of others. Therefore, turning all negative thoughts into positive workmanship." And Brenda's observations about how her small group had been working: "It shows me a lot of school spirit," she had written after watching a videotape of her classmates' work, "and a positive attitude of each and everyone's personality." Selene agreed: "Some people have changed through all this study of Boston." "They are learning that they can talk in front of the class if they knew that everyone was a friend."

It was hard to reconcile the students' commitment to their writing in and on drama with the concerns that the principal was outlining about the declining standards in literacy. I found it difficult to understand how her emphasis on workbooks and practice books would encourage, as she believed, the children to write in complete sentences. "We've seen a degeneration in their handwriting, and a degeneration in their speaking and writing in complete sentences," she claimed. Handwriting was going to be taught formally next year to combat this problem. I thought, What role would drama have in this new curriculum? Drama as a teaching tool for calligraphy? But isn't there a danger that such a formal approach to writing might thwart the students' passion and conviction? Albert had revealed both qualities in the following entry, written in role as an imprisoned soldier during the period of the Boston Massacre:

> I'm in great and horrible pain. Sorrow settles in the pit of my heart. My anger rocks my very brain. Life's meaning has been lost through the past few months. We are in enemy camp, prisoners of a deadly war, one which we are in obvious disadvantage cause mother Britain knows not of the colonies' rebellious attitude. We are the beginning casuelties, framed by the sly acts of this dirt-infested Boston. It ridicules mother Britain's Boston.

The faculty meeting was coming to a close. What a good weekend we were all going to have as we contemplated who was going to get sacked! I gathered my papers and journals, noting the letters the students had written as American patriots describing for a friend their encounter with a Tory spy. Even Meryl had submitted hers. These kids are great, I mused. They give me such strength. Standing up, I heard the principal saying something about summer book-lists and how every student had to have enough summer reading to keep "busy" over the holiday. She reminded us to check the display of student homework assignment books so decisions about which one to select for next year could soon be made. A colleague asked whether anyone had noticed a peculiar buzz with the fire alarm bell the previous week. "No, not me," I answered, thinking that I should be more interested.

There was no discussion. No department or interfaculty meetings about curriculum or the welfare of individual students. There never seemed to be any time, particularly now with all the money problems. One faculty meeting a month meant that there was always an enormous administrative agenda to wade through.

I helped rearrange the classroom back into the familiar rows of desks, noticing the "Study for Success" sign on the bulletin board as I did so. I wondered what the reaction of the other teachers would be if I erased *Study* from the sign and changed it to *Drama*. "Drama for Success," now there's a thought! I returned to my eighth-grade homeroom to collect my plan book and my map of eighteenth-century Boston. I made a meager attempt at tidying a few papers on my desk, and prepared for the usual fifteen-minute walk to the rat-infested subway. I winced when I glanced at the time. It was already 5:00 P.M.!

The school, principal, and teachers described here are real. They existed in time and space, and I existed with them for a twelve-month period; no doubt others like them are in existence across the country. The previous account is a familiar one: overworked teachers and principals, administrative chores and a daily school routine to contend with, economic burdens and their impact on curriculum programs. The demands on teachers seem overwhelming to me as I reflect on this account—especially how these demands are compounded when teachers, like myself, challenge school hierarchies by embracing process drama, a nonconventional and artistic mode of learning.

As I now read over that account, written a few years back when I worked in that school, I am intrigued that the information it provides is not so much directed at what happened in one particular faculty meeting but tells more of my own relationship to that faculty meeting. There is a sense of the writer's alienation from the principal's need to canvass the urgent matters of the day—matters pertaining to student discipline, student notebooks, and general teacher-student relations. I am intrigued by my own distance from, yet engagement with, the events happening around me, by the wanderings of my mind to Meryl, by my desire to leave and get on with my drama planning, and by my occasional need to challenge the principal. Perhaps if Meryl had not responded assertively in the drama on that day I may have had quite a different perspective on this faculty meeting. If I had experienced management problems with a difficult class, for example, I might have had another response to the principal's agenda. My context shapes the meanings I generate. My state of mind, my recent experience, my understanding of people and events, influences the manner in which I construct meaning.

Readers might equally be drawn to my estrangement. Maybe you share the experience of teaching in an elementary or high school where the administrative and economic concerns of the officials are in contrast to the immediate classroom happenings of your students. Perhaps you cannot escape from your context either. Your environment shapes your perception, and your response to events, such as faculty meetings, are determined and influenced by your context. Forty students in a classroom might well be an administrative solution to a financial crisis, you may assert, but it is teachers and their students who bear the brunt of this decision.

Alternatively, some readers, who might be principals or administrators, could be annoyed by the smug sense of self-assurance that I have conveyed and regret that I revealed no interest in the daily organization of this school and appeared unfairly critical of school operations. "It is all very well for teachers to complain about the bureaucracy," might be this reader's response, "but jobs are dependent on the school's existence." No school, no job. License is given to take any action necessary to ensure effective management and to preserve ongoing employment.

How is it, I wonder, that different meanings can be given to the same moment by different people? How is it that sixteen elementary school teachers in one faculty meeting could have different interpretations of that one event? How is it that an incident can be constructed in radically opposing ways? Can we ever construct a truthful version of the same incident? How does the context in which we work shape what is possible and what is not possible?

Introduction
Understanding Context and Taking Charge

This book is an examination of my values toward a particular method, in this case a mode of teaching, and how that mode can be provided for and managed within a particular educational context. It is important that these values be exposed from the beginning. My interest in drama education has been an evolving one, growing over a twenty-year period of teaching at elementary, secondary, and college levels in the United States and abroad. In that time, I have worked with many of the documented leaders in the field, most notably Dorothy Heathcote and Gavin Bolton (1995), David Booth (1994), and Cecily O'Neill (1995). Their joint interest in negotiated drama, in which the teacher and children coconstruct an imaginary event as a way of understanding some aspect of their lives and the world around them, spoke powerfully to my own interest in shaping an artistic work based on all the participants' experiences. But I also understood that this shaping occurs within a particular classroom environment, where teacher and students bring to drama their own cultural perspective on life and learning. While I was drawn to experiment with the strategies of teacher-in-role, tableaux, forum theatre, and whole-group drama as developed by these great leaders, I realized that my attempts at repeating others' work were useless if they were not to account for my lived professional context.

How is it possible, for example, to introduce process drama within a school environment where lessons are forty minutes long and there is a standard traditional curriculum? How do teachers accommodate a principal's need for taught handwriting skills when drama is their preferred mode of working? How can the stated academic requirements of the school be balanced with the desire for

1

artistic endeavor? These are questions I struggled with when I found myself teaching social studies in an environment where my fundamental beliefs on education were brought under intense scrutiny. This book describes my journey.

ABOUT THE PLAYERS

Meryl: A Seventh-Grade Student and Her School

Meryl was twelve years old. She was quiet in class, although verbose with her two friends, Nadia and Jessica. She was born in Spain and had attended the school since second grade, unlike her two friends, who were Italian Americans and born in New York. These three girls seemed to get on very well together and would often work as a group. They did not mix all that well with their peers, however, and I wondered whether there was some racial tension given that the majority of students in the school were Asian American.

Although I had to contend with a forty-minute subway ride and the frenetic peak-hour rush, the daily trip home for Meryl involved crossing the street and taking an elevator ride in her high rise. I initially envied this convenience. The majority of the children, like Meryl, lived in the housing-commission apartments in the immediate neighborhood. When they were dismissed from school, many of the children would have to attend after-school programs or cope with domestic chores such as cooking the evening meal, tending to siblings, and other household tasks. Where would these junior high students find time for the required two-hour homework? Perhaps this might be left to the morning before the domestic routine began again. Parents worked long hours, usually in factories or restaurants. I believe that some children only saw their parents on weekends.

Unlike Meryl and her friends, close to 85 percent of the children attending the school were Asian American. Most of these were part of a second generation. A visitor to Meryl's school in the 1920s would have observed a very different cultural population: the children of recently arrived Italian immigrants. The school had been founded by missionaries intent on providing spiritual and educational relief for this cultural group. However, the demographics had changed notably. Although the community still had an Italian base (the school pastor, for instance, was Italian, as were many school board members), the original cultural identity had dissipated. At times, it appeared that the school had difficulty accommodating the new ethnicity that the Chinese had brought. For example, the Chinese New Year was not formally celebrated in the school; also, the children were expected to participate in parochial services even if they had a different religious identity. Meryl and her two friends, being Catholics, were ironically in the cultural minority within a Catholic school.

There were other social and familial ways in which Meryl was different from the majority of her classmates. Her Chinese-American classmates, for instance, lived in extended families, frequently with grandparents who were charged with rearing them. When a family representative of the Chinese-American student came to school for conferences, it was usually a grandparent. If the grandparent spoke no English, the student would be present to translate. Teachers tended, as a rule, not to request these interviews because of the perceived inconvenience to the families.

For Meryl, Jessica, and Nadia, there was immediate nuclear family support and no hesitation by the school administration to call in the families. Their parents were more actively involved in the affairs of the school and I presumed this fact was because they spoke English, which gave them a decided advantage in the participation of school life.

For all of the children, though, the routine of the day was the same. Meryl and her peers were expected to be in the classroom by 8:05 A.M. for "morning exercises." Since the school was positioned on top of a church, on the sixth and seventh floors, they had to climb six flights of stairs and regularly came into class short of breath. The "exercises" consisted of a prayer, the pledge of allegiance, and the singing of the national anthem. Classes commenced at 8:20 A.M. exactly. It was not uncommon for the principal to be on the sixth or seventh floor at that time to check that students were working. This work usually meant that teachers would be engaged in "formal instruction." The typical empty vessel approach to learning would neatly characterize this school environment. It was common for classrooms, except in the kindergarten, to be arranged in rows of desks. Students were generally told where to sit. The teacher's desk tended to be in a prominent position, often at the front.

Meryl and her class faced six consecutive "lessons" before their noon lunch break; fifteen minutes of the latter would consist of "recreation" in the yard. The grueling morning schedule met with some relief in the afternoon when classes resumed at 12:45 for 2:30 P.M. dismissal.

In the seventh grade students felt the looming presence of the eighth, and therefore they had tremendous pressure on them to succeed academically. Coming from my eighth grade to work with the seventh graders in social studies, I was often struck by the home-room teacher's constant reminder to her students between the les-son changeover period of the sacrifices that their parents were making to send them to this school. A huge brown-and-gold ban-ner, "Study for Success," adorned a bulletin board in the rear of the classroom, the same classroom where the faculty meeting described in the preface took place. The homeroom teacher for the seventh grade would alert her class to this banner frequently. The class rules, which emphasized cooperation, courtesy, obedience, and good work habits, were in full view.

Although Meryl was reserved in discussion, she was assertive when I privately asked her to describe a typical social studies class. This description was important to me because I wanted to get an idea of the manner in which social studies had been experienced by children in this school. "We would be talking about climate and about the world," she said. When I asked her about the kinds of classroom activity she was used to, she explained that teachers "would tell us to read from the book and then they would give us some notes and questions, and then she would call for answers, and that's really it." No wonder she would later add, "It really wouldn't be that interesting."

The social studies textbook Meryl referred to, *The Challenge of Freedom* (Sobel et al. 1982), was noticeably well worn and out of date. The textbook was organized into periods of conventional his-torical periods, chronologically arranged from the Indians to Watergate. The tasks asked of students demanded the most limited intellectual endeavor, usually that of recall. The teacher's edition of the textbook contained the "answers" to the questions and cited further textual material that could be "dictated" to students.

From Meryl's observations, it appeared that her previous social studies teachers would mechanically work through the chapters, setting the assigned reading and questions. When Nadia, her friend, later added, "We read the chapter, then do the questions, then have a test," a view of learning in this school was being confirmed. The picture the group described of a typical social studies class was reminiscent of the late Paulo Freire's "banking" concept of education, "in which the scope of action allowed to the students extends only as far as receiving, filling, and storing the deposits" of the teacher (1970, 58).

I was struck by the mechanical manner in which Meryl and her fellow students described the deadly routine of their social studies lessons. It seemed to me that they had been schooled into accepting a monotonous drill, one which left them complacent, if not apathetic, about the educative role of social studies. I was saddened that they had not had an opportunity to experience the excitement of collecting and interpreting data, or had faced the struggle of formulating accurate and logical judgments of historical events. If ever there was a group of kids who needed to have some energy injected into their social studies curriculum, here it was.

For this reason, I decided that the seventh graders would benefit if they experienced social studies from a more active point of entry, an entry point powered by process drama. As Meryl's class was split into two separate groups for social studies, the challenge of documenting one group's work from as many different student perspectives as possible seemed manageable. Meryl's social studies group consisted of twelve students, some of whom you've met already. The others you will meet in the next chapter. The other group consisted of twenty-three students.

Meryl's group is the one that informs my discussion. This focus is purposeful given the consistent negative characterizations of social studies which Meryl's group articulated at the beginning of our work together. I saw it as my professional responsibility to challenge these negative stereotypes and to provide a contrasting learning encounter. But in getting launched into the process drama with the students, there was a more pressing concern that had to be addressed.

Meryl's context of learning was far removed from the collaborative and negotiated one that I advocated. The fact that there was no mention of group work other than answering textbook questions posed an immediate dilemma: How do I introduce process drama—a group-centered, contractual activity—when the students' experience of social studies is characterized by passive, solitary, and inevitably mechanical tasks? To what extent can process drama as a learning tool be used in a school dominated by a conservative and transmission model?

Philip: A Seventh-Grade Teacher

My teacher-education years in Australia had emphasized that the pursuit of knowledge was not something that could be neatly packaged in a box and impressed in young people's minds. Knowledge as dictation lesson, I was told, implied that the learner was a passive recipient, who moronically overdosed on the half-baked truths of others. My mentors had insisted that we had for too long been massaged by the notion "Education as narcotic: submit and enjoy!" "How can addiction be empowering?" they would ask. Addiction is a vice; it deadens the will, usurps the power to control. The firm diet of Dewey, Rogers, and Holt provided the theoretical basis. The arguments were impressive and formative: Knowledge could not be transmitted but rather had to be created and re-created from the perspective of the learner. In Gordon Wells' description, knowledge had to be "constructed afresh on the basis of what is already known by means of strategies [that individuals] developed over the whole" of their life (1986, 218). And strategies are developed both in and out of school.

When I commenced teaching as a twenty-one-year-old in Australia, I had trust in my mentors. The implications of their teaching had major ramifications on curriculum planning. Students needed to be engaged in their learning in an active fashion. Consequently, there would be much group work and collaborative projects. The schools I worked in were committed to the notion that children not only learned in groups but as groups. Drama, by its very nature a group activity, became part of my being as a teacher. My education in drama helped in the teaching of other subjects. Teachers consulted on an interdisciplinary level, projects were shared, and release time was given for preparation and inservice work. There was little supervision, plan books were not rigidly kept and inspected, and people got on with the job.

Times change! In my early thirties, I took up a position at a school in a country that gave birth to the great educationalists whom my mentors celebrated. Was it not Dewey who said nearly eighty years ago that a new movement was sweeping through education that would focus our attention from the teacher to the student? "The child becomes the sun about which the appliances of education revolve; he is the center about which they are organized" (Dewey 1921, 35). I recognized from the first day, however, that the shifting center of gravity that Dewey predicted had not swept through this school. One of my first log entries captures my reaction to this shifting center:

> I met the grade seven homeroom teacher today. She suggested I
> prepare a bulletin board for the children on the first day. This was
> all very new to me. "But they're big kids," I quietly contemplated.
> She suggested that as I was the social studies teacher I could do
> a big red-white-and-blue bulletin board. She had a copy of the Pre-
> amble, Declaration of Independence, and Constitution that I
> could pin up. I appreciated the generosity but felt uneasy
> for some reason. I asked about the possibility of organizing the
> kids' desks into tables. She didn't think this was a good idea
> because the "children would goof off." She gave me a copy of the
> school rules and recommended that I go through them with the
> class. I feel enclosed in this place, almost like I've entered a
> prison. This is not a healthy start, Philip. Remember when the
> door shuts it's your classroom. Just you and the students.

Six months later, I had a better feel for the school. The teachers were all committed to children even though they operated in their classrooms more traditionally than I did. I regretted that there was little time to chat. Although we might see one another briefly in the faculty room over the lunch break, they would be busily feeding children's multiple-choice test sheets into the Scantron machine for correction. Like *yard, Scantron* became a familiar term associated with this school. My colleagues often wondered why I did not share their enthusiasm for multiple-choice tests. "It cuts down on the paper load," the seventh-grade homeroom teacher would frequently say, while watching me reading yet another pile of student essays.

CRITICAL THEORY AND
RADICAL PEDAGOGY

When I wrote the log entry in the previous section, I was engaged in more reading, writing, and thinking about school than at any previous time. Before this time, although I had been involved in subject and professional associations and had been to numerous conferences, I had participated in these events from the perspective of a teacher who wanted to learn more. But I found that in the ever increasing frequency that I would go to these meetings, I was really not developing more sophisticated skills. Although I was receiving more activities to do with my kids in the classroom, my ability to think about how to structure these activities in a logical sequence, or how to construct dynamic curricula, was based on what others told me to do, rather than on information I generated for myself. I felt that my capacity to think intelligently in my classroom was very much determined by how that intelligence had been directed or groomed by those who seemed to know more.

I could always tell as a teacher those who knew more: Those who knew more wrote books, worked in universities, led workshops at conferences, had done research, and had assumed leadership positions on important bodies. Those who knew more were articulate and lively speakers, appeared to have a breadth of knowledge on many topics, and were very popular. I found that I could not get enough ideas from those who knew more. I was usually the first to subscribe to seminars that they conducted and prided myself on my ability to make direct contact with them so that I had privileged access to learn more.

But ironically I later discovered that the more I learned the less I knew. On my return to school, after having learnt from one who knew more, I would amaze my classes with yet another exciting idea or activity. My kids always could be assured that when Mr. Taylor came back from a conference, a seminar, an inservice class, or a graduate class, they would experience another great idea; there was usually one great idea each month. My intentions, of course, were in the best interest of my students. I liked teaching and felt that the kids liked me. But then something different happened. I started reading about such phenomena as teacher-based inquiry, action research, and the reflective practitioner. This reading was all new to me and terribly challenging. It seemed to contradict my need to learn from others. It emphasized the importance of teachers' activating their own classrooms as sites for critical inquiry and understanding the context in which they worked. I was encountering for the first time the hostility many teachers expressed toward mindlessly accepting the ideas of those who knew more. Did I fall into this mindless category? Was I an unintelligent practitioner who used my students as guinea pigs so that I could try out a new idea?

I began reading about critical theory and radical pedagogy and encountered the ideas of Giroux (1988), McLaren (1989) and Kincheloe (1991). Here I discovered the resistance toward much academic research that failed to communicate to those practitioners grinding away, every day, often at six hours per day, with large groups of students. Here I was challenged to think about how my teaching reinforced powerful hierarchies and promoted the interests of particular groups. Was I really disempowering students in my classroom when all my intentions were to be good with them?

At the core of teacher research, it seemed, was the belief in the capacity of educational leaders to activate their ability to think intelligently within a classroom context (see McLaren and Giarelli 1995; Brunner 1994; Cochran-Smith and Lytle 1993). Yet, the critical teacher researcher would understand how this context was constructed and would recognize how power relations are formed. I wanted to be a teacher-researcher, but I moreso wanted to be a *critical* teacher researcher: Who wouldn't? I wanted to break down the barriers between myself and my students and explore issues related to power, control, and equity. I wanted to revitalize the classroom as a legitimate site for educational inquiry. I was excited by this prospect, given my own cynicism about academia, and decided that within a particular school environment I was going to take charge of my classroom and do some research! This book documents that experience of taking charge.

Many of the books I read on educational research are unhelpful because they lean toward theoretical exposition at the expense of locating theory in context. Although policymakers and others in charge of creating regulations for large groups supposedly have the best interests of teachers and children at heart, it is the individual stories of practitioners at work within their own communities that move and educate me. I am reminded of Nancy Atwell's *In the Middle* (1987) and Lucy Calkins' *Lessons from a Child* (1985), which richly describe how two teachers radically changed their teaching through intensive participant-observation. Their stories speak to me because they are located within a context. I can see and hear the students' voices, and I empathize with the teacher who is challenged to make direct changes to teaching based on immediate observation.

Similarly, the case studies of teacher research edited by Bissex and Bullock (1987) and Goswami and Stillman (1987) have had a powerful impact on how I work with kids. Is this to do with the manner in which these works are grounded in actual classroom experiences? Does it have something to do with the real-life struggle that teachers face daily in their school community? Might an answer to these questions lie in the authentic classroom contexts that are so vividly communicated and that richly resonate with the experiences of a large cohort of teachers and their students?

THE STRUCTURE OF THIS BOOK

In this book I will focus on how the authentic contexts in which we work influence a teaching and learning encounter. My aim is to share with readers my experience of introducing a variety of drama strategies and techniques in the social studies classroom with children who had no prior experience with drama. I will explain how this experience shaped my ability to reflect critically on what makes for good teaching, and I will present numerous examples of classroom incidents in which I have consciously changed or modified an approach so that my students, like Meryl, can engage with the work. I shall describe episodes of collaborative inquiry in the social studies classroom and the circumstances that gave birth to them. I will tell of the many writers and movements that have informed my own classroom pedagogy. Although most of my illustrations will come from my social studies classroom and how drama was incorporated into it, I suspect that educators outside this field will share an interest in how deliberate attempts at classroom research can enhance the quality of teaching and learning.

At the outset, I'd like to make clear my own researcher values. I am a firm advocate of the qualitative approach to research, an approach that honors the voices of classroom participants and hails, as its motto, the tenet of "less is more." The experiences governing the observations contained within this text are those driven by one group of seventh graders and their teacher's encounters with process drama. This case-study approach is a deliberate one. While there are many textbooks that describe how to teach drama and the various strategies and techniques open to teachers when they plan to implement drama, there are few books that take a reader through the actual daily experience of real children when they encounter drama. I figured that it would be more useful for teachers with little background in process drama, the principal audience for this book, to read about how a process drama can evolve in action, and what factors affect a teacher as students respond to the work.

Process drama is a dynamically realized event, and for some it can be intimidating, especially when leaders have to rethink their aims in action and improvise on the spot. This book hopes to debunk the intimidation by recapturing how a class inexperienced in drama activity, with their teacher, can be transformed from passive, inert individuals to thoughtful and activated beings. As a qualitative researcher committed to rich, descriptive accounts of human affairs, I believe I can demonstrate this process more completely by focusing on a moment in time that I experienced with my seventh graders, rather than by covering a range of different lessons focusing on different themes.

In this respect, I began our journey with a description of the environment in which process drama occurs. The contexts in which we teach are powerful. Every school community has its own cultural, social, political, and economic makeup, a phenomenon referred to as "cultural capital" by the Frankfurt School, a research network that formed in Germany in the 1920s and that was critical of conventional approaches toward research activity (see Doyle 1993). Cultural capital is a useful concept because it assumes that each group is by nature going to be fundamentally different from any other group. The cultural capital of my students posed certain issues in relation to my ability to investigate. My teaching identity is determined in relation to the cultural capital of the school community. The cultural capital of my students and the context in which we worked and how this influenced my initial attempts to introduce drama in the curriculum will be taken up further in Chapter 1, "Process Drama and Cultural Capital."

The many demands placed on teachers often preclude their ability to inquire into how effectively they are educating their students. Although the description I gave in the preface is from my own elementary school teaching and indicates an evolving philosophy on teaching and learning and how this affects my students' understanding, it is not an unfamiliar one in schools across North America, Australia, and Europe. Frequently teachers tell tales of how their desire to introduce an innovative and dynamic approach is constrained by the educative climate in which they work. The increasing paper load, bureaucratic impositions, and the pressure to achieve outcomes not only prevents teachers from experimenting with new ideas, particularly drama ideas, but also stymy their ability to describe their experiences. Teachers' capacity, for instance, to act as critical and self-conscious investigators is thwarted when others outside the day-to-day classroom happenings are entrusted with devising school policy, promoting models of classroom practice, or advocating particular instructional approaches. Chapters 2 through 4 identify process drama's different educational orientations, and how these orientations give rise to numerous curriculum and reflective possibilities. In the past, some commentators have argued that process drama just facilitates learning across the curriculum and does not promote learning in and about the dramatic art form. These chapters debunk those mythologies that emphasize the pedagogical component of process drama only. Process drama does more than service the curriculum; it creates a curriculum, and it does so by generating an art form that teachers and their students learn to manage and implement.

Chapter 2, "Understanding from Within," describes how the demands of the dramatic art form promote understanding from inside the experience. Drama strategies such as teacher-in-role, tableaux, and whole-group negotiation which can facilitate contemplation and reflection are recorded, as well as the important function that reflection in action plays. Chapter 3, "Shifting Perspectives," explores the power of the dramatic art form to challenge people's understanding. The chapter demonstrates how drama strategies were introduced to achieve objectives in a social studies curriculum, and the impact that these objectives, achieved through process drama, had on the learning context. I will describe how conceptual understanding is a complicated phenomenon and cannot be readily quantified through standard measuring instruments. In process drama, students are enacting roles and experiencing dynamic moments. These moments can place huge demands on the participants, and in this chapter we see how these demands influence the teaching and learning possibilities. Chapter 4, "Building a Knowledge Base," focuses on the knowledge base that the teacher and the students are generating in relation to process drama, and how this knowledge base can be structured and developed. The growing control that the students and their teacher have over the dramatic art form is documented, and the ways in which process drama affected their views on curriculum are examined.

Perhaps the demands on classroom teachers are no more evident than with the national curriculum initiatives that have recommended standards and competencies (Consortium of National Arts Education Associations 1994). In the United States, the Department of Education had set as one of its goals the achievement of high standards in American schools. Although it is significant that the National Assessment of Educational Progress (NAEP) had included the arts on the list of subjects to be assessed, I wonder how these decisions affect the work of teachers? To what extent, for example, do national standards assist educators to examine critically their own practice? How do federal calls for nationwide measurable competencies contribute to the educators' ability to generate knowledge on teaching excellence and effectiveness? How can educators remain adept to examining their own practice so that they can improve their classroom performance? Chapter 5, "Reflective-Practitioner Research," proposes a model for teacher research in light of the competing needs to balance community, state, and national education priorities.

The concluding sixth chapter, "The Future," highlights the often unrecognized potential of process drama in the curriculum, an arresting force that can provide our children with a voice and a forum through which they can demonstrate their knowledge and evolving understanding of the world. The stories of kids and teachers experimenting with process drama will be recalled, as will the plea for more grounded studies that yield the evidence so often demanded by administrators, parents, and community leaders when attempts at advocacy are made.

1

Process Drama and Cultural Capital

In recent times, the term *process drama* has been gathering increasing momentum as a useful description of structured improvisational activity in which teachers and students jointly contract to an imaginary world. The aim of this contract, like the aim of any significant artwork, is to reveal in some clearer way the nature of the world in which we live. By participating in an imagined world, by stepping into the shoes of someone else, we are provided with opportunities to transcend the ordinariness of our own lives as we contemplate what might be possible as we aspire for clarity and meaning.

The work of the British educators Dorothy Heathcote and Gavin Bolton identified a particular mode of working in drama that valued the importance of human learning.[1] Rather than focusing primarily on the skills being taught, such as speech and communication, or the content to be studied, such as theatre history and dramatic criticism, these leaders concentrated on the quality of the experience for participants when they enter or contract to a fictional context. What happens to classroom participants when they release their imaginations through improvisational activity? What kind of learning might occur as teachers and students act out roles and situations? How can leaders most effectively press students' thinking and understanding when they pretend to be others?

Heathcote and Bolton would enter classrooms and, with their student participants, cocreate a fictitious world where ideas, values, attitudes, and visions could be interrogated and transformed. These fictitious worlds might center on historical themes as a vehicle for pressing the students to accept some responsibility for their actions and for their evolving beliefs. For example, when dealing with the subject of political cover-up as demonstrated through the Watergate scandal, Heathcote enrolled students as museum curators creating an exhibit. The curators imagined they were wax models who must teach the public something about the complexity of Watergate (Heathcote and Bolton 1995, 86–87). Through the process of creating and becoming wax models, a drama strategy referred to as *making tableaux,* students considered what powered their interest in Watergate and how that interest could be shared with others. In another process drama, which focused on Arthur Miller's play *The Crucible,* Bolton enrolled the students as families of puritans who must deal with the possibility that their daughters might have been engaged in immoral acts (Verriour 1989). Here, Bolton took on the role of a minister, a drama strategy known as *teacher-in-role,* which allowed him adeptly to challenge the puritan families (the students in role) on how they would deal with the evil presence in Salem.

While Bolton and Heathcote did not originally describe their work as process drama, preferring to use terms such as *improvisation, drama in education, educational drama, drama structure,* and, more generally, *drama,* their approach has been influential, especially with language arts and social studies teachers who could begin to see a valuable way of incorporating drama into their curriculum.[2] This approach challenged dominant understandings of drama in schools, understandings that often centered on games, exercises, and performed plays.

I am indebted to Cecily O'Neill, who has helped clarify the genre of drama activity we now refer to as process drama. Process drama can be distinguished as a genre of drama activity by its:

- focus on improvisational activity jointly constructed between the leader and the group
- emphasis on using dramatic artistry to help students confront some aspect of themselves and of the world in which they live
- concern with imagination and thematic development

- indebtedness to the Heathcote-inspired approach, which values the importance of reflective learning
- use of theatrical techniques that assist contemplative involvement, such as teacher-in-role, tableaux, and dance-drama
- focus on what is happening now rather than on what is happening next

Sometimes this structured improvisational approach has been described as drama for learning or drama in education, descriptions that highlight the shifts in understanding or meaning making that the participants develop. Not only do historical themes lend themselves to this mode of working but a range of contemporary issues, stances, and questions can be explored and interrogated through process drama. In O'Neill's (1995) Spaceship Omega drama, for instance, students project themselves into the role of futuristic NASA scientists who have to contend with a spaceship, Omega, which has suddenly returned after a long absence. The astronauts on Omega have not aged, and are now faced with the prospect that their families have changed and perhaps have forgotten them and established new lives. In this drama, students are confronting the struggles of those faced with uncertainty and possible emotional trauma in their lives. Drawing on similar themes, David Booth, a Canadian teacher of process drama, inducted a group of sixth graders into the roles of islanders facing the potential barbarism of soldiers plundering their land for its loot and treasures (see Taylor 1995b). Here, the student participants are faced with issues of imperialism, privacy, and public violation.

In each of these cases we see an emphasis on exploring some aspect of our world and how we live in it. However, one difficulty in claiming this approach solely as "learning" is that it has led to a confusing notion that the art form is somehow devalued or that artistry isn't being emphasized. A few commentators have argued that a process drama approach is an antitheatre one because there is little formal study of theatre history, acting, and direction, or alternatively that students are not engaged in the process of devising or working on written scripts for production purposes. From the outset, we need to be clear that such a distinction of drama from theatre is not a helpful one, for it implies that process drama workers are operating from a nonartistic perspective. In the Watergate, Crucible, Omega, and Islander dramas, for example, it is the art form and how the participants operate it that generate the learning.[3]

If process drama is to achieve its full potential, then teachers need to be working with a finely developed sense of theatre practices, and they need to hone their conception of art and artistry. It is important to note that process drama operates from a different tradition than the American creative drama school.[4] Creative drama is often concerned with story dramatization; students are cast into roles and reenact plot lines. There is little deviation from a predetermined scenario, and often the effectiveness of the work is judged by a group's ability to mimic or reenact a story faithfully. While process drama might be inspired by a written story, the meanings that the group generates from the story are the focus, and the relationship that students demonstrate to the story is the main concern of the leader and group. The plot is not as important as the group's ability to probe what sense they are making of it. In this respect, the process drama worker is always interested in what is happening now as opposed to what is happening next. The former concern releases the leader to explore how students are positioning themselves at any given time around the artwork created. The latter concern emphasizes linear development and may prevent the participants from opening up to the full possibilities of the artwork they are creating.

THE HUMAN CONTEXT
OF LIVED EXPERIENCE

Teaching curriculum through process drama can be one of the most exciting and powerful ways for leaders to work. As drama puts students on the inside of an imaginary event, allowing them to look at the event from the inside out (e.g., as eighteenth-century Bostonian patriots deciding on the tactics needed to curb the growing redcoat menace), they are provided with an immediate personal voice because of the direct nature of the experience.

There is now considerable evidence that when children experience drama in the curriculum they are more in control over their own learning. Recent anthologies by B. J. Wagner (1998), John Somers (1996), and myself (1996), document the growing volume of studies that demonstrate the power of drama in children's lives. The research convincingly reveals that drama can help student participants generate control over their curriculum knowledge. I also recognize, though, that the word *drama* can raise anxieties among teachers and students who have a negative predisposition toward it based on prior unhappy experiences or stereotypical notions of what children might be doing. I am reminded that one of the early writers in drama, Caldwell Cook (1917; see also Allen 1979, 11), was much criticized by his colleagues for having his language arts students sitting on desks from which they "dangled" their legs. Cook was eventually told by one principal to "stop all this nonsense."

Sometimes participants new to drama anticipate that they will be engaged in behavior that is publicly embarrassing or that personally threatens them in some way. It can therefore be advantageous to avoid using the term *drama* given its connotations with groups who have no direct experience of this way of working. Such avoidance was a priority when I first worked with my seventh-grade social studies class. I knew that they needed to be protected from a too-public demonstration too soon. I needed to find a secure and comfortable way of launching the work.

Start from the Students' Context

A long white strip of paper with colored markers placed on it had been laid out diagonally across the room. We were on the floor positioned around the paper, as if we were about to eat an important meal. Tom, Albert, and Teddy were lying on their stomachs, apparently grateful to be out of their desks; others, like Nadia, Jessica, and Meryl, sat cross-legged, speculating on what might be in store for them that lesson. Selene, Madelene, Amara, and Susan were quietly kneeling, waiting, it seemed, for the teacher to speak.

There was a nervous energy running through the group as it was unusual for them to be out of their desks at all. Something different was about to happen. "I thought," I tentatively began, "that today we would share with each other our views of how we see learning as happening. When do we learn, for example? What moments in our life can we remember having learned something? If we had to draw a picture of someone learning, what might that picture be?" I asked the class to draw or write whatever came into their minds when they thought of learning. A few, like Nadia and Jessica, frantically started to write, almost as if they were being tested. Others slowly followed. I gradually noticed the frequency with which "school," "teachers," and "books" seemed to come up; learning did not seem to be something, in their minds, that took place outside of school.

"When you think you've finished, have a look at what others have done, and if you feel like it add things to theirs," I said while moving around the room. Joyce and Amara were busy drawing pictures of chalkboards and textbooks. Joyce and Amara, Chinese Americans, were two of the more reserved members of the class. Their home-room teacher explained to me that often the Chinese American females were reluctant to contribute because of the submissive role they were expected to play in their homes. Furthermore, she thought, the fact that I was a male teacher, one of only two in that school, might have influenced their willingness to participate. I was unsure whether I should accept the cultural and gendered stereotypes of this teacher, but given my inexperience working with this school, I thought it wise to reserve judgment.

Amara, a petite girl with jet-black hair, had recently turned thirteen. Later in the process drama, she confessed that except for in social studies class she was rarely asked for her own ideas in school. This was a reason, she claimed, why she was so silent in class: "Sometimes I can't think of any ideas." The textbook, in her mind, had been presented as the source of ideas, but she felt often "you think differently from the book and have more ideas to it . . . different ideas from the book." The power of book learning in this school was pervasive in the images the group was depicting: *memory, homework, dictionary, vocabulary, words,* and *brains* were terms Amara listed.

I noticed that Joyce had written *must be done immediately* above Amara's *homework*. It suggested to me something that either a teacher or a guardian had frequently said to her. Joyce was twelve and a half. I thought at the time how tiny she was for her age. She appeared to like the traditional aspects of school, such as writing and reading, and she was reluctant to participate in discussions unless invited. I wondered whether the culture of the home or the culture of the school had promoted this habit? Her father, she told me, held down two jobs. She had many taxing domestic duties at home. I recognized that financially things were tight for her family. Like Amara, she rarely went out after school or on weekends. Both families, it seemed, were concerned about the growing violence in the neighborhood.

The activity confirmed my own suspicions about how learning had been presented to these students in the past. I noted the recurrent responses. Learning to this group meant:

Study
Smart
Read
Thinking
Pens
Listen
Answer
Concentrate

Although some mentioned "talking," "helping one another," and "doing the best you can," these observations were infrequent.

The cultural capital of this group appeared to be informed by a transmission model of learning, a model that values the teacher's role as the primary instrument for producing knowledge. These students did not see themselves as the generators of their own learning but rather as the receivers of mine. It seemed that they had conceived their role as passive recipients who recycled the ideas of others. This kind of information was important to me in the early phases of the work because it provided the necessary evidence of the children's cultural context. Cultural, in this sense, refers to the myriad of social, environmental, and habitual elements that comprise human identity. As a teacher I am more informed when designing a learning experience when I have some understanding of what values the students will bring to it. Also, knowing their values influences how I shape curriculum learning. In general, understanding students' cultural context demands that the leaders are interested in the following sorts of questions:

- How do my students show what is important to them in education and what is not important?
- What models of learning are these students familiar with?
- Why do these students support particular models of learning?
- What experiences have these students had of teaching and learning, and how can I begin to transform some of these?

When teachers can probe the cultural contexts of their students, they will begin to plan learning events that respond to and acknowledge the life experiences of all those participants who come to educative events. By monitoring the students during this first phase of the process drama, I faced the question, How am I going to move into dramatic activity, an enactive mode, given the sedentary and passive perceptions of learning that the group has?

Gathering Data on Group Dynamics

It seemed important to find an activity in these early stages of the process drama that would not expose the group too early. I needed to avoid an activity that would make them feel threatened. The worst scenario, to my mind, would have been to begin work with this particular group with the words, "Right. Today we're going to do some drama!" I assumed that for these kids, the more I could do to allay their anxieties the better.

Building on the group's observations of their own learning, I asked them to work in small groups to devise two or three still-life physical representations, or tableaux, of how children learn. One of the advantages of a physical depiction of an event, action, or incident is that it "releases" participants from the demands of immediate action. The group was not asked to improvise or act out an event, but rather to create a "freeze-frame."[5]

Although their enacted images of learning were not dissimilar from their projected ones on paper—their focus on teachers was common in both, for example—it was fascinating to observe how the small groups reached consensus about what to devise. By monitoring how the children worked, I was noting how well they collaborated together and how their ideas germinated. This information, I figured, would be invaluable as the process drama developed. The decision making in one group, for example, seemed to be less than democratic:

NADIA: One [of the pictures] could be the kids reading. One could be happy about what he is reading and another could be the kid bored!

JESSICA: Another could be shocked.

MERYL: Like looking around the classroom.

JESSICA: Meryl could be shocked. Like with a big expression on her face.

NADIA: That's two. Another one could be a bunch of kids raising their hands. Yeah! Okay, you [Jessica] be the teacher for one. I'll be the teacher for another one. And he [Teddy] is going to be a teacher for another one. The first one is going to be all the kids reading with their teacher. The second one is going to be the kids taking notes.

MERYL: You could have the teacher like writing on the board.

JESSICA: And the last one could be the kids raising their hands and the teacher picks him.

NADIA: Yeah, okay! Let's do the reading one. All right everybody get a book. Except for the teacher. All right you [Teddy] sit up here.

PHIL (to the whole class): If you want to change something in your picture do so.

NADIA: Not everybody can be bored.

Nadia's presence in this group was felt by every member. I knew Nadia to be a mature, confident, and expressive student, but it was interesting to watch how dictatorial she was in this activity. Although she was best friends with Meryl and Jessica, this relationship did not deter her from being authoritative with them.

Nadia, a thirteen-year-old Italian American, was the second oldest girl in the class. She was tall and heavyset, had long brown hair, and regularly contributed to class discussions; her physical dominance over the other students seemed to provide her with considerable status in the group. She later confessed that, unlike Joyce and Amara, she did not enjoy the traditional aspects of schooling, namely reading and writing, much preferring the active encounters of group work. She once exclaimed, "When I see in class that no one is answering the teacher's questions, I think, 'I'll answer them!'" She appeared perceptive, comfortable with adults, and discussed a range of current events.

Jessica, also of Italian descent, was one month younger than Nadia. Jessica and Nadia were very close. They regularly phoned each other out of school, and shared mutual interests, including fashion, boys, and music. Schoolwork was a chore for Jessica. She would later tell me how she disliked the routine and regime of homework, which she often complained about. She was an attractive and friendly student who, like Nadia, conversed easily with adults.

Meryl would "hang out" with Nadia and Jessica although she was the youngest of the three. She had long blond hair, was tall for her age, and, like her friends, was physically mature. She, too, admitted disliking schoolwork. I noted her difficulty in meeting deadlines. Once she wrote that she enjoyed drama because "It gives me a chance to be the center attraction. It lets everyone participate + tell them some ideas." In the group talk shown here, however, she had difficulty impressing the other two girls with her suggestions.

Teddy, on the other hand, was not heard at all. Having recently turned twelve years old, he was the youngest in the class. A slightly obese and eager student, Teddy appeared completely swamped by this group. I assumed that being a male and the only Chinese American in the group might have been the reasons for this reaction. However, I needed to be careful that I wasn't layering my own gendered and cultural stereotyping on him. He willingly followed Nadia's instructions, a move that tended to reflect his cooperative and submissive demeanor.

Watching all the students working on their tableaux, I searched for a role-context, a fictitious forum, through which these pictures could be shared. I needed to help them look at each other's work critically and reflectively. I hoped this role-context would be a vehicle for us to explore the past. Who, I asked myself, might be interested in photographs of children learning? Historians, of course. Historians of the future interested in the past! By asking myself the right kind of question I naturally fell into a potentially dramatic encounter. Our process drama was about to begin.

PHIL: Ladies and Gentlemen, I thank you all for coming to this twenty-first-century exhibit on life in school two hundred years ago. This year we are excited by our collection of photographs we've uncovered from an intergalactic vessel. We think these pictures depict a school in another orbit, perhaps from another hemisphere. I personally think the school was located in a place called [the location of the students' school]. I'm not exactly sure where that is but it keeps coming up in our history books as a dark and undesirable location in another galaxy [laughter]. As interested scholars of past schools, I'm sure there might be something of interest to talk about after we go through the exhibit.

Right, stopping there. Who do you think we were? Who might you have been?

NADIA: People of the future!

MERYL: Looking back!

PHIL: If we use our idea of being people of the future when we share our photographs, do you think you can be those people of the future looking back?

While the photographs were being shared, I saw my function as supporting the contributions of the "scholars" as they analyzed and speculated on the qualities of learning. Interestingly though, I was unprepared for the silence that ensued, especially since the group had generated the content of the pictures.

My growing frustration led to a volley of teacher-imposed questions, which made the futuristic meeting redundant. An encounter of the strained kind is evident in the following discussion about the groups' tableaux:

PHIL: Tom is the expert on this picture, aren't you?

TOM: No!

PHIL: Well I do recall how the other day you said, "Hey, look what I found out about schools back then!" [To Tom, hoping he will accept] What do you think this [first] one is showing? [He doesn't accept. After what seemed like a minute's duration] If you look at this person in the photo [referring to Teddy, who is sitting at the side], he is the only one not reading. Who might he be?

TOM [Reluctantly]: The class clown. The teacher.

PHIL: Why is the teacher not reading? [No answer] Okay. Let's have a look at the second one. [The group in this photograph assumes their pose; it depicts a class of seated children raising their hands.] Now, time-warp scholar Susan, you're the first one who noticed this picture, aren't you? [She nervously nods. Silence] That's right. What would you say this one is revealing about learning back in those days?

SUSAN [Hesitantly]: That they seem to be very anxious to answer the teacher's questions.

PHIL [Gratefully]: Yes, that they seem to be very eager . . . eager beavers answering the teacher's questions. What would you say about the teacher? That the teacher was interested or not?

SUSAN: She was asking a question.

PHIL: How is this photograph different from the previous one that we saw? Would you say that the teacher is different in this one?

I had thought that the tableaux would be a useful bridge into our first drama encounter. My casual confidence, however, that adequate preparation had been given quickly dissipated when I was met with the students' reluctance, hesitancy, and nervousness. My own anxieties grew. As the dialogue shows, hoping to salvage what I was now perceiving as a significant miscalculation, I specifically approached Tom. He was one of the more outgoing members of the class.

Soon to be thirteen, Tom, a Chinese American, was a handsome lad, tall for his age, and strongly built. He was popular with his fellow students, particularly the boys because, it appeared, he would tease and aggravate the girls. Although I figured that he might inject some interest in the drama and thereby help the others find a voice, the closed nature of my questioning actually disempowered him. I panicked.

I next appealed to Susan for assistance, but as I signaled that I was the teacher instead of elevating her role's expertise as the scholar, her responses, like Tom's, were strained and unaccepting. Where had I miscalculated in the structuring?

Susan, although occasionally reticent in class, was an intelligent, sensitive student who seemed to enjoy school. She was heavily built for a thirteen-year-old girl, and often came to class moody. She admitted feeling that teachers made her believe that there was always a right/wrong answer. It was apparent in this encounter, for instance, that she feels burdened with a sense of "what am I supposed to say?"

How a leader questions in role was of concern to me here. I felt that I was demanding too much from the group—that they were having to do all the work. I was not helping them create a context for the pictures. I was expecting them to be able to do that by themselves. I canvassed alternative approaches to the whole-group drama. "Perhaps," I mused to myself, "if in the supervisor's role I suggested seriously flawed interpretations of the pictures or assisted with their own analysis, the students might have started to create roles for themselves." Sometimes taking a devil's advocate role can help draw the group into the imaginative world. Although the students had an inclination to be reserved in discussion anyway, it was still evident that structuring a drama by simply asking questions was insufficient.

The sharing of photographs, however, reinforced the dominant role that teachers have in the students' perceptions of learning. It was, therefore, misguided to think that through one dramatic activity I was successfully going to challenge these ingrained perceptions. From nine pictures, though, it was significant that there was only one that didn't have a teacher as a central figure.

In that picture, Tom and Susan were grouped with Selene and Madelene. The four of them were sitting in a circle, apparently having a discussion—a different encounter from the transmission model of learning depicted in the others.

Selene was the youngest girl in the class. I would later refer to her in my log as "the cone of silence" because of her reluctance to speak, and I would become increasingly concerned by her silence. It was characteristic of Selene's family, her homeroom teacher was quick to explain, that they would be bashful and introverted. Selene later wrote that her favorite classroom activities were *silent* reading and journal writing. It was ironic then, that her group tableau contrasted with her own preferred learning proclivities.

Madelene, on the other hand, was more extroverted, often contributing to group activities. Drama, she later confessed, was enjoyable to her because it helped her understand "more" about a subject. Unlike Selene, she disliked writing in her notebook and journal. It seemed appropriate that she would be in a tableau in which collaborating with peers was emphasized. Madelene was tall for her age, almost thirteen, and she often mixed with Susan outside of school.

Matching Context to Planning

A predominant feature of process drama is the manner in which leaders reassess teaching and learning strategies both before and during the structure. My immediate and reflective reading of participants' actions and reactions would influence the choices to be made, the direction to be followed. Richard Courtney's disclaimer that a "map is not the territory" (1997) echoed with penetrating accuracy. How foolish, I thought, it would have been to preplan the entire process drama given the backgrounds and temperament of the group.

Although I was disheartened with certain aspects of the initial structuring, it was clear that a foundation for more significant inquiry was being laid. The group had been introduced to two key elements of process drama, tableaux and teacher-in-role; they had collaborated in different groupings, small and whole group; they had shared a rich array of material on the theme, learning; and, they had created a potentially useful role-context for entering the past, as people of the future. These latter two points suggested rich possibilities for future structuring, as my log, written like a dialogue with myself, indicates:

> Learning now? Learning in the future? What about Learning in the past? We know that the People of the Future have uncovered pictures of Learning now. What if pictures of children learning in a distant time period were found? In our social studies classroom we are about to study Boston society in 1770, especially this event known as the Boston Massacre where British soldiers were accused of shooting on innocent American patriots. How, I wonder, would children have learnt back in those days? If you work with the idea of being expert scholars on the past, how can you use the Space Convention and pictures of learning in 1770 as a way into the theme of revolutionary society? Important to vary the task; you don't want another tableaux so soon. What would happen if a document was found, perhaps related to this Boston Massacre? Possibly connect this document to the children in some way so that a direct link is being made to their pictures of kids' learning. You need to help build their commitment more directly to the future people though. Ask them to reflect on the pictures as futuristic people. Yes, write a report to a supervisor.

As a consequence of my log musings, I invited the students, in role as conference delegates, to write a report for their supervisor on the space convention they attended. These supervisors' reports, as they became known, were the first written task the group engaged in, and they aimed to help the students generate a role that would drive and inform the action.

There was a wide range of responses when these reports were read aloud, a further indication of the varied levels of students' talents, interests, and observations. Brenda, the oldest girl in the class at thirteen and a half, wrote the most succinct account:

> In the conference I learned that most photographic exhibits are taken place in school. Most of the picture has to do with reading, and taking notes. It also has to do with desire in learning during the school season.

Although she comments on what some pictures revealed and hints at a personal attitude to them (e.g., "desire in learning"), the writing task does not appear to have helped strengthen her role as a "person of the future." Little indication is given of the perspective from which this piece was written. Perhaps the general de-emphasis on expressive/poetic writing in the school and the fact that students would not be penalized if they decided against completing the writing were factors here.

Brenda, like Selene, was one of the more introverted Chinese-American students. She hardly spoke during class. Her disengagement from activities was often evident by the way she would sit on the sidelines. It was difficult to read how Brenda was reacting to the work because she had an expressionless demeanor. She kept to herself. I later learned that her family was in arrears at the school, which meant that Brenda was not able to receive report cards or sit for tests until the debt was paid. This was a new policy the principal had instituted to combat the financial predicament of the school. It was difficult knowing what impact this public knowledge had on her character.

To my surprise, later she admitted enjoying the role-playing activities, particularly because they enabled her to understand concepts more clearly. "It's easy to visualize them," she once said, "than thinking what would happen." Writing, however, even through the guise of role, was viewed as a chore.

Albert, on the other hand, wrote an extraordinary report. His penetrating views on the "oppressive" teacher who watches in judgment and his command of his own role as an observer of "the very simple [twentieth-century] school life," are reminiscent of a student much older than his thirteen years. I quote this piece in its entirety, keeping intact the author's original style.

Dear Supervisor:
 My attendance to this meeting has not been fruitless. The director, Mr. Taylor, brought me around to view astonishing pictures of school life. Those 20th century people had very simple school life. In one picture, barely comprehensible, a teacher was viewing the children with a observant eye determined to be in control. This was called "Teacher's Eye on Students," a rare picture taken at a moment's notice. Other pictures depicts an authorative figure, stress: one directing and leading the children's education. For ex, the "Participation," "Learn By Looking," and "Student's Obedience." In the first one, teacher gets to pick student to participate in some activity, presumably some oral answer, a question pertaining lesson,

or a permission to do something. In the second one, students seem to be copying problems of the teacher who is writing on the 20th century antique called the blackboard. It showed a boy, 1/3 of total students (the others female), in a relaxed and undignified fashion, seemingly uncaring of education. Other students weren't that attentive either. It showed a fault in that system of teaching, the student's interest was not captured. In the third one, students were writing what the teacher dictates. Other photos showed pictures like the "Study and Concentrate," and the "Free Talk." These show a independent reading work and a class discussion. In the reading work, they were into it and seemed to enjoy a bit of private time, while in the other, they seemed happy to open themselves up and speak with the rest. In all, it showed different activities which students engage in. The ones with teachers made me feel quite oppressive, with a teacher watching everything and leading a child's education. Somehow, I don't like those teachers because I can easily distinguish them from the pack and that proves to me that the teacher was not in the group or part of the group, though in the other pictures, they were more friendly and had a lighter atmosphere.

The manner in which Albert had grouped and provided titles for the photographs indicated a conceptual grasp not widely evident in the others. Albert, a student with a slight build, was, as this piece indicates, an observant, thoughtful, and mature student. If I had misplaced an item, for example, or was concerned about something, Albert would often predict how the problem could be solved. Although he appeared self-conscious about his height, he was not ostracized by his peers. He related very well with Tom and Teddy and seemed not to care very much for the girls.

Given the breadth of approaches to the in-role writing assignment, however, I was faced with what persisted as a recurring challenge: making the tasks carry some meaning. How does the writing structurally assist the development of the process drama? What forum will enable all participants to share their work in a valuable way? How will the group accommodate and empower such a vast range of approaches?

Although our work in these early stages had generated an enormous number of questions about perceptions of learning, about the participants, and about the process drama, I thought these would inform my own planning and thinking as a social studies teacher. At the same time, I knew that I would need to address directly the social studies curriculum in which we were operating.

THE CURRICULUM AREA: SOCIAL STUDIES AND PROCESS DRAMA

While I was gathering data on the group's dynamics, I was reminded of the curriculum context in which I was working: the social studies classroom. Some background on this context is required before I continue. Social studies is an area of the curriculum that appears to hold many rich possibilities for process drama in that it can quickly put participants on the inside of an experience.[6] However, although drama is sometimes suggested as a possible extension activity in social studies textbooks, there is very little evidence that teachers are using it. Indeed, within my own classroom context, my kids were presenting a picture of social studies that seems to be an all too familiar one in the life of students

For instance, Albert once wrote that in the past he was sometimes reluctant to contribute in social studies because he had been conditioned to answer teachers' questions and "not have conversations" with them. Even though he was friendly with his previous homeroom teacher, he still found it "hard" talking with her because he was "so used to teacher-student type of talk." In sophisticated terminology for a thirteen-year-old, he described this difficulty as "a crippling disadvantage with modern education system." When I later asked him to elaborate on this idea, he confessed that he never initiated dialogue with teachers; his role was "to answer them." He would never challenge teachers' authority, even when he disagreed with their stance. The fear of a grade penalty seemed to be the rationale for this anxiety. As I talked with other students about this, however, it was clear that although grades influenced their readiness to participate, other more powerful factors seemed to affect classroom interaction. These centered on the nature of the social studies curriculum itself.

Frequently, the students would describe classes preoccupied with notebooks, copying from the board, and, as Nadia asserted, other "boring stuff [such as] . . . listening to the teacher talk about what is in the book." The book, the power of the written text, was common in their observations. "We read from the pages," Madelene insisted, "keep our notebook, and she gives us questions to answer." Curriculum as "object" appeared to be the unanimous view of what went on in social studies. There was no mention of more interactive-centered projects such as group discussions and small-group work. There was certainly no mention of drama. If, as I believe, curriculum is rooted in "discourse, dialogue, action, and interaction" (Clarke 1989, 375), this was not the model with which these students were familiar. Albert's observation, "crippling disadvantage," reverberated in my mind.

The social studies textbook the students worked from, *The Challenge of Freedom*, (Sobel et al. 1982) was a massive eight-hundred-page tome. I noticed how Chapter 8, on the Boston Massacre, followed a similar framework to the other thirty-nine chapters: chunks of text interspersed with a few pictures but pivoting on key comprehension questions. The questions for Chapter 8 characteristically aimed to test factual recall:

Why did Private Walker go to the ropewalks?

What groups of people were involved in the fighting during the weekend?

Why were Samuel Adams and many other colonists opposed to the Stamp Act?

What did the Quartering Act force many colonists to do?

When did fist fighting first break out between Boston ropemakers and British soldiers?

In what ways were the Bostonians and the British troops similar?

Why did the guard at the Custom House place a bayonet on his musket?

What did the man in the red cape appear to be doing?

Who ordered the soldiers to load and fire their weapons?

What verdict did the jury reach in the trial of Captain Preston and his troops?

Who was the first person killed in the Boston Massacre?

How many people were killed and wounded in the Boston Massacre?

Why were British troops finally removed from Boston?

Rather than asking students to interpret, play with, and re-create the material, the tasks demanded the most limited intellectual endeavor, usually that of recall. Students were expected to find the correct factual answer listed in the textbook. Not one question appeared to require an analytical stance. History was being presented as a set of controlled absolutes that were not open to question. Reading the list, I was reminded of the words of Thomas Newkirk:

> Even students who can accomplish the important comprehension tasks such as locating the main idea, summarizing and drawing inferences are controlled by the written language if they must accept the writing on its own terms, if they lack the power of questioning the integrity of the texts before them. Lacking this power, they are only deferentially literate; they are polite readers. Like good guests they do not ask impertinent questions. (Calkins 1982, 10)

From the students' observations, it appeared that their previous social studies teachers would mechanically work through the textbook's chapters, setting the assigned reading and questions. No wonder the curriculum had been viewed as "crippling" and "boring," considering the closed, distant, and parochial nature of the presentation and questioning. Teachers who hope to enliven their social studies classrooms, Parker (1991) argues, need to try "an array of methods" and decide which of these "with different kinds of content has a clear advantage" (1991, 17).

A report on the state of social studies education condemns the traditional focus on memory recall and rote learning prevalent in many schools and recommends an approach that will

> shift the emphasis from the mastery of information to the development of fundamental tools, concepts and intellectual processes that make people learners who can approach knowledge in a variety of ways and *struggle with the contradictions* [emphasis added]. (Verhovek 1991, B4)

A question I would ask later in my logbook, "What constitutes knowledge in social studies?," would become a recurring concern. If, as Freire (1970) asserts, knowledge "emerges through invention and reinvention" and not through regurgitation, how can learning opportunities be structured for this to happen? This concern is especially important in learning environments like the school context I am describing, where the transmission model is dominant.

Duckworth (1987) suggests that in traditional classroom environments children are usually accustomed to providing teachers with "the quick right answer" (64). These students sometimes have difficulty accepting classroom situations in which their own values and ideas are emphasized. When knowing "the right answer ahead of time" is viewed as more important in school than "ways of figuring it out," then challenging these perceptions can take time.

In process drama, though, teachers are attempting to help groups generate and create their own reading of the work. However, as Heathcote (1971) argues, problems arise if the "sequence of communication" in the drama is such that the teacher "signals" a correct reading or, alternatively, expects too much of a public contribution from the group too soon. As shown here, the messages I was sending to the seventh graders in the early phases of the process drama were mixed ones. I was expecting them to suspend willingly their disbelief and enjoy the experience of creating an imagined world, yet, at the same time, when their reactions were not as I anticipated, I quashed their role taking with a frequency of teacher-dominated questions. The teacher, therefore, needs to be easygoing, unprejudiced, and, as Heathcote claims, "receptive" to multiple readings, "helping the situation by receiving, challenging, helping to develop ideas and above all creating and preserving in the class attitudes of receptivity, non-value judgments and artistic integrity" (50).

THE FRANKFURT SCHOOL AND CULTURAL CAPITAL

As I have begun to reveal, process drama cannot function unless it accommodates the contextual frames that the group inhabits. This is one reason why process drama is such a challenging genre of drama activity, because it demands collaborative and negotiated involvement between the teacher and the students. In this book, *contextual frames* refers to the socially and culturally constructed meanings that teachers and their students bring to any educative event. These meanings might focus on:

- *Ethnicity and Race:* What constitutes our ethnic and racial identities? How might these identities influence and shape our responses to process drama? To what extent does our identity exist beyond ethnicity and race? How is identity constructed?
- *Social, Economic, and Familial Backgrounds:* How do my students interact with one another, and how do I interact with them? What models of group dynamics seem to operate in my classroom? Where do our ideas about family and society come from,

and how are these presented in the classroom and the process drama? How do our ideas of society and community impact how we interpret and understand ourselves and one another?

- *Personal and Educational Experiences:* What do my students teach me about what is important to them? What do I teach my students about what is important to me? What are our interests and hobbies? Why do these students attend school, and why do I teach in school? What should we both be getting out of school? What are our educational expectations? How might drama accommodate these expectations?

These contextual frames could be likened to the cultural capital of the group—that is, the psychological and physiological makeup of the participants. My seventh-grade class, consisting of predominantly Chinese Americans, had views on curriculum, learning, and drama that are specific to their own context, even if other classes might share these views. In the Introduction we saw how the context of the school and the principal influenced what these students would bring to their learning. A traditional parochial school that centers the power in the teacher's hands and that is based on strong discipline affects how the learning environment is perceived. Likewise, in the early phases of our process drama work, I must ask myself, What are the students' own contextual frames? How do the students demonstrate what is important for them? What kind of classroom experiences do they value? How do they read the function of the teacher?

As I look beyond the content of curriculum material, I ask myself, What drives this content? What are the values that inform the content? What do I hope students will do with the content?, I am beginning to operate from what some have referred to as a critical theory perspective. The acknowledgment of where the students are coming from and where we, as the leaders, hope to take them, forces us as teachers to ask direct questions about whose interests are being served when we are educating young people and about what is worth knowing. These are the kinds of questions critical theorists ask. When my students demonstrate to me that the major model of teaching and learning that they have experienced is based on Freire's banking concept, what kind of challenges does that pose to me as I begin to introduce process drama?

For instance, the fact that my students were reluctant to participate in the in-role drama in which the photographs were being shared perhaps says little about their attitude to drama itself but more about their confusion about how this approach relates to education. Students who have been provided with few opportunities to use drama in the curriculum may naturally come to the view that drama is not an officially sanctioned and therefore legitimate way of working. This belief may have little to do with whether drama is of benefit, but more with their perception, a perception informed by the events that have shaped their cultural capital.

Critical theory has emerged from a particular approach toward educative thought known as the Frankfurt School, a school of thought said to have developed in Germany in the 1920s. In this theoretical framework, rather than teachers recycling with their students the truths of others, they ask, Where have these truths come from? Whose story of reality is being promoted? When you know whose story is being promoted and valued, you can begin to critique whether or not this story might be representative of other people's stories.

As I was to discover in my social studies classroom, there had been very few opportunities for my students to examine how knowledge was constructed. For the most part, my students had been put into the role of consumers of others' knowledge; they were never encouraged to probe whose interests are being served by the perpetuation of particular truths. In other words, the power hierarchies that have led to specific views about our world and how we live in it had rarely been challenged. Because a critical theorist responds to and recognizes how the human dimension constructs ideas of truth from the circumstances in which that dimension is housed, questions about power, knowledge, and meaning are always at the forefront. Process drama, given its social and cultural construction, inevitably emerges from a critical theory framework. And this framework poses a number of complex challenges.

For instance, I knew that the primary responsibility for launching the process drama rested with me. As O'Neill (1991a) says, "These [teacher] decisions will include selecting or negotiating the starting-point . . . taking on a role, endowing the participants with roles and structuring the development from within"(3–4). And while I intended that these decisions would be made jointly between teacher and students as the work proceeded, the challenge would be to ensure that my initial planning would contain a kernel of interest for the group and suggest possibilities for future group planning.

I wrestled with the notion of taking a document from the pre-Revolutionary period and playing with that through some role. I knew that the social studies curriculum demanded that we examine Boston, a linchpin of tension between the colonial and patriotic forces, but I was unsure of what constituted a "core of entry" into this period. An event known as the Boston Massacre appeared to convey many of the antagonistic forces that led to the War of Independence, yet I was troubled by the idea of having the group read reams of material as a preparatory step.

My log entries capture some of these concerns with this initial general planning phase:

> What constitutes knowledge in social studies?
> What information can I assume the group knows about Boston
>   during pre-Revolutionary times? Maybe if I could find a
>   forum through which they could ask questions about the period.
> How to do this so that it isn't typical teacher questioning?
> How do I incorporate reading into the process drama?

Through the course of suggesting and discarding possibilities in my log, I contemplated the following:

> Perhaps starting with an event is the wrong way in. The choices
> might be easier if I knew something more about the group. I seem
> to be making a lot of judgments about how they learn: through
> questioning, writing, reading. How do *they* think they learn? Have
> I ever asked them that?

I knew I had found a possible "core of entry," and as the students began to describe and create their images of learning, the seeds for an investigation into a past event became clearer.

When teachers begin to ask questions about what they hope to achieve and why, they are acting in a professional manner. But when they ask whose interests are being served from such a study, what values are being reinforced, and what do they want students to do with this knowledge, then they are asking questions within a critical framework.

Process Drama and Critical Theory

As process drama hinges on the leader's ability to respond to the contextual frames in which groups find themselves at any particular time, it demands that leaders develop the capacity to act as critical theorists. And this may be one reason why process drama has been such a controversial medium among some authors[7]: It questions and challenges dominant understandings of what schools are for and what we should learn in them. Perhaps a further illustration might clarify what it is I understand about the stance of a critical theorist and how it shares a common perspective with process drama.

I remember with great clarity one of the most powerful learning moments for me as a teacher. It was the experience of working with Cecily O'Neill and a group of American graduates at The Ohio State University during a summer session for a weeklong process drama based loosely on the idea of a fringe group searching for a better place in this troubled world. This idea was one crafted by the group, including the leader, but as the participants committed deeply to the fictional context, as they constructed the context of those on an expedition to a better world, some were not prepared for the hardship they faced—hardship to do with survival, with violation, and, finally, with their willingness to sacrifice all memories of their past life in return for everlasting knowledge.

The dilemmas encountered were powerful, and the group experienced states of fear, anxiety, and excitement. It seemed to be one of those moments in a process drama when the boundaries between fiction and life were overlapping, and participants were confronting or grappling with some revelation about themselves and the world they lived in. How can I release a memory of a loved one? Is my dream for enlightenment more important than such memories? For a moment in time it seemed that the group had not just been transported to another world through the process drama, but were also transported beyond and above themselves, where they could pay witness to their own values and the values of others.

In this respect, not only does process drama operate on the same principle of good theatre, which explores the kinds of people we are and the kinds of lives we live, but it also works on a principle of revelation familiar to the critical theorist. The process-drama worker and the critical theorist are committed to inquiry and exploration; both aim to help participants confront truths and to probe individual and group meanings.

What the group then does with the truths uncovered varies according to which theoretical position one is influenced by, and the kind of outcome one is seeking. Just as some critical theorists have argued that hierarchies and inequities should be exposed and marginalized, so some process-drama workers have wanted to relate knowledge to revolutionary action. Ultimately leaders will have to decide for themselves what they hope students might do with the knowledge they generate. For my own preference, I am more sympathetic to an orientation that honors artistry and imagination. Like O'Neill, I believe in the individual's capacity to construct meaning for himself or herself, and that if we believe that art forms are truly transforming then teachers might respect their work better by letting it speak for itself rather than suggesting a course of action that participants might pursue. This is another reason why O'Neill is such a wonderful teacher: She places her money on the art form, and on the human capacity to engage with it, rather than depending on any editorializing that some leaders might feel compelled to make.

This stance, however, does not mean that leaders do not develop a particular curve or ethical position on the material. After the "People of the Future" meeting with my seventh graders, which I described earlier, I contemplated a possible approach to the American revolutionary period. When consulting a curriculum document for guidance, I noted that the overall objective of studying this period was to "understand how colonists' concerns regarding political and economic issues resulted in the movement for independence" (The State Education Department 1987, 42). This objective was daunting in its explicit statement of what students should "understand." I sarcastically mused in my log, "So much for freedom of thought!" There seemed to be one view of understanding —a status quo view if you like—the conventional wisdom, which students were expected to recycle and not question. I was not satisfied with this approach as it appeared to prevent multiple and diverse views on the event. It seemed more in line with a pedagogical orientation that prioritized predetermined outcomes, an orientation lacking in its critical perspective.

The list of "model activities" proposed to help achieve that objective was also disappointing. The activities focused on having students answer particular questions on why taxes were introduced into the colonies and how they were received: "Why did colonial spokespersons not accept British concessions? Why did the colonial leaders not yield ground when Parliament rescinded some of its laws?" And later, "Have students read short excerpts from *Common Sense*, by Thomas Paine. Have them report on how this book convinced so many people that separation through war was necessary"

(42). What an uninspired litany of activities. Social studies was again being presented as the "mastery" of information (4). Although paying lip service to the development of conceptual thinking, it appeared that this task was being construed as old-fashioned book learning. This approach seemed tied into Hirsch's (1987) view of cultural literacy, wherein individuals must have at their command a body of propositional knowledge prescribed by the dominant cultural group. A critical theorist would challenge the worth of such a view, and would hope that students could generate their own ideas rather than simply be cast into a position where they were meant to moderate the position of others.

Likewise, my interactions with my students challenged me to consider what a study of social studies might and could entail. I began to develop a working definition that would help us confront the revolutionary period:

> I like this idea of social studies being stories of time. Stories neatly encapsulate the idea of breadth, variety, contrast. After all, stories of the same time might be told differently depending on who is the storyteller. History textbooks often don't think in terms of stories, but rather dispassionately recount the known "facts." But what are the known facts? An Iraqi mother attempting to comfort her young family during the constant battery of fire during the Persian Gulf campaign might tell her grandchildren a version of those events unlike that of her American counterpart in Brooklyn, New York, the latter glued to the 24" TV screen with its smart bombs and patriot missiles! Similarly, a family member who has lost a loved one because some lunatic has shot down a group of primary schoolchildren in a Scottish school, or visitors to a national park in Tasmania, Australia, will have quite a different perspective than someone reading about it for the first time in a newspaper. Our stories often develop from the angle in which we position ourselves around an event, the angle of our repose. To get a handle on history I believe is to understand the power of story.

I began to hope that the students would eventually become storytellers, each having his or her own narrative to share. There is now growing literature on the power of narrative in students' lives, and the role the storyteller has in the shaping and construct of knowledge formation (see Bruner 1986; Bruner 1994; Hillman 1983; and

White 1987). If I could assist the students in creating their own story on an event, in the process would they be confronting the question of whose values are being celebrated?

It was this notion of storytelling that drew me to an engraving of a pre-Revolutionary incident known as the Boston Massacre. The name, Boston Massacre, was given by the patriot, Sam Adams, to an incident that occurred in King Street on March 5, 1770. On this day, the official textbook story maintains, a small number of British soldiers were called out of their barracks to quiet down a fever-pitch crowd. The riotous crowd was seeking revenge after a British sentry had reputedly assaulted a youth. Sam Adams later maintained that the soldiers deliberately provoked the crowd to disquiet. Consequently, when shots were fired by the "lobsterbacks," an insulting term that the patriots, particularly the "liberty boys" (gangs of youths), teased the soldiers with, Adams attributed this gunfire to the willful aggression of the British. Five colonists were killed in the "massacre" (Sobel et al. 1982, 140). The picture that Adams had circulated in the town has become a classic portrait of this incident: the ruthless, calculating, and bloody-minded officers lined up in a single file shooting mercilessly upon the victimized crowd (Figure 1–1).

I began to understand why the patriots would embrace this picture as a symbol of their oppression. The punishing effects of British occupancy were clearly conveyed. Adams was attempting to tell a story, and he selected an evocative means of doing so. This picture is striking in its one-sided presentation of the event. The oppressive presence of George III is suggested by the billowing smoke of the soldiers' musket fire. This picture seems archetypal to me: It is on a level with any seductive image. What is surprising is that an archetypal propagandist portrait might seem more fitting to the Third Reich than to a relatively small-scale uprising in eighteenth-century America.

The trial of Captain Preston and the soldiers responsible for the shooting indicated that it was Adams's oppressors who saw themselves as victims. The soldiers had a very different story to tell from that of the patriots (see Kidder 1870). Their story focused on victimization, provocation, and crowd harassment.

I was excited by the challenge of developing our own story of the Boston Massacre. The incident presented an array of conceptual issues worthy of exploration: How do we arrive at a truthful version of the events? Whose cause, the patriots' or the soldiers', has

FIGURE 1–1 *Boston Massacre in King Street, Boston, March 5, 1770. Engraving by Paul Revere. Courtesy of CORBIS-BETMANN.*

greater claim? What does the Boston Massacre say to seventh grad-ers? Where would we position ourselves, if we could, in Adams's picture? As I chose to ask these kinds of questions, rather than the ones posed in the students' textbook, a critical theory framework was emerging. I hoped that students would be able to step back from the event itself while, ironically, at the same time stepping into it. The trick was to find a focus in the process drama that would put us on the inside of the revolutionary world so that our own narrative would develop and our voices would be released. That focus is the subject of the next chapter.

NOTES

1. Heathcote and Bolton are the two foremost English pioneers of a school of drama praxis, now referred to as process drama. Heathcote studied theatre in the Northern Theatre School in Bradford, with Esme Church and Rudolph Laban. Now retired, she lectured for thirty-six years at the University of Newcastle-upon-Tyne, and attracted students from all over the world. Her work has been the subject of books by Wagner (1976) and Johnson and O'Neill (1984). Bolton lectured in drama at Durham University from 1964 to 1989. He has been especially influential in the field of drama education and has said that Heathcote's approach to drama teaching transformed his understanding of drama and education in the early 1960s. Because Durham is geographically close to Newcastle, Bolton was in a privileged position to observe Heathcotes's praxis evolve over her formative years. He has published numerous books on process drama (1979, 1984, 1992, 1998) and, like Heathcote, has been responsible for training many of the current leaders in the field (including David Booth, Michael Fleming, Cecily O'Neill, and John O'Toole).
2. Compare later Heathcote articles with an earlier piece (1967) on improvisation, a term that guided her thinking in the 1960s.
3. Michael Fleming's (1997) book, *The Art of Drama Teaching*, helps clarify the relationship between dramatic form and process drama.
4. Winifred Ward (1930, 1952, 1957) is the acknowledged American mentor for the creative drama school.
5. See O'Neill (1995) for a more comprehensive description of this strategy, especially pages 126–128. As O'Neill writes, a tableau task "releases participants from the demands of action, requires deliberate composition, embodies understanding, manifests meaning, allows time to be frozen or recalled, permits a level of abstraction to enter the work, and shapes and shares both information and insight" (127).
6. See Fines and Verrier (1974) for an early account on the power of drama in the teaching of history.

7. Those readers interested in tracing the debate might usefully begin with David Clegg's (1973) article published in *Theatre Quarterly,* in which he claimed that a sole emphasis on *structured improvisation* in school has denied students access to a critical theatre heritage. This view was one later developed by David Hornbrook (1989) and Peter Abbs (1994), who were both of the opinion that process-oriented approaches to drama lacked an artistic-aesthetic framework. What Hornbrook and Abbs failed to account for, though, was that artistic meaning-making occurs in process and that artworks are not just artifacts demonstrated through such objects as a school play or a formal study of theatre history. As stated earlier, British pioneers like Dorothy Heathcote and Gavin Bolton reconceptualized drama curriculum with an emphasis on participants' change in outlook rather than on their ability to demonstrate an array of theatre skills. Their work has been influential throughout the world with leaders in Ireland (Fitzgibbon 1997; Fyfe 1996); North American (Booth 1994; Morgan and Saxton 1996; Tarlington and Verriour 1991; Wagner 1976); Australia (Carroll 1996; Hughes 1991; O'Toole and Donelan 1996); and Scandinavia (Eriksson 1995; Heikkinen 1997; Rasmussen 1996), promoting a process view that highlighted the transformative and revelatory possibilities presented by drama praxis.

2

Understanding from Within
Learning in Process Drama

THE CHARACTER OF LEARNING
AND PROCESS DRAMA

I am of the view that learning and process drama are inextricably linked and that such linkage occurs in a complex, dynamic way. The complexity of process drama and learning is tied into the particular demands of the dramatic art form, and the difficulties one faces in conventionally reporting upon an artistic event. There have been some commentators who have questioned the very nature of learning and process drama, arguing that the claims that are sometimes made for its power cannot be convincingly held. In the next three chapters, I'd like to make a counterclaim: It is very easy to illuminate the kinds of learning possibilities generated by process drama and to describe how teachers and students experience these possibilities.

While not wanting to set up artificial barriers between types of learning, I think it is helpful to distinguish between the approaches, or orientations, toward learning and process drama. These orientations can be rationalized in three ways: (1) learning in process drama, which refers to what happens to students when they are caught up in the event of making, presenting, and reflecting in drama; (2) learning through process drama (examined more fully in the next chapter), which refers to the conceptual knowledge students are generating about themselves and their world as a result of their experience of process drama; and (3) learning about process drama (explored in Chapter 5), which refers to what leaders and students believe process drama can teach them and how they might more effectively manage the art form in the curriculum.

Let's begin our discussion with the following encounter: Placing a desk in the rear right-hand corner of the room I asked the group, in role as supervisors, "Where might your desks be in relation to this one?" Hurriedly and with much exuberance the supervisors positioned their desks. It was a chaotic arrangement, vastly different from the ordered rows they were used to. Tom moved his desk immediately next to my own. Leaning sideways in his desk, he mischievously put his feet up on my desk, much to the amusement of Albert and the other members of the class. There was a sense that permission was being given for them to act in ways not usually sanctioned in this school. I offered a narrative link: "The Superdupervisor [the name the group gave my role] sent word around the intergalactic office that he had discovered some very interesting information. Word had it that a very important meeting was going to be held."

The meeting would present the supervisors with an odd document. Unbeknown to the group, the document was actual testimony by William LeBaron from the trial of the British soldiers (Kidder 1870, 57–58). LeBaron's deposition was one of ninety-six statements solicited to suggest that the soldiers incited the 1770 riot. Note in the following extract how he focuses on the soldiers' harassment of the "liberty boys":

I, William LeBaron, of Boston, of lawful age, testify and say, that on Monday evening the fifth day of this instant March, about ten minutes after nine o'clock, being in King Street with my brother Francis LeBaron, saw a soldier, the sentry of the Custom-house door, running after a barber's boy; the boy called out as if he was in distress, and the soldier pursuing him with his firelock, told him if he did not hold his tongue he would put a ball through him, after which the soldier returned to his post; immediately after this I heard a great noise in Silsby's lane, so called, and immediately about thirteen or fourteen soldiers appeared in King Street, near the watch-house, with their drawn swords, cutlasses, and bayonets, calling out, "Where are the damned boogers, cowards, where are your liberty boys;" at which time there was not

more than eight or ten persons in King Street; one of the soldiers
came up to me, damned me, and made several passes at me with a
drawn sword, the last of which the sword went between my arm
and breast, and then I run, as I had nothing to defend myself, and
was pursued by a soldier with a naked bayonet, who swore he
would run me through; at which time your deponent called fire!
and soon after the bells rung and further your deponent saith not.

As I had reflected on this passage before class, I had writtten in my
log: "There's a story to be told about these lads who the soldiers
describe as "boogers" and "cowards." How did they get the name of
liberty boys? Why were they such an irritant to the soldiers? Possibly the group could devise an incident that suggests how the liberty
boys received their name?"

In class, the Superdupervisor explained that while he felt he had
uncovered an exciting find, he was unable to understand what it
meant. He appealed to the expert scholars for assistance. The scholars, too, had never seen language like this before. "What does the
soldier mean by 'put a ball through him'?" Albert asked. "A ball?"

Meryl mused, "a bullet perhaps, through his head or something.
It's an expression. He wants to scare the boy away so he wouldn't
do anything to him." The document was replete with unfamiliar
words such as *firelock, cutlasses, naked bayonet,* and *deponent.*

Some supervisors examined the context of the words so that they
would be able to uncover the meaning. "I think," Meryl proposed,
"*deponent* means like leader or captain because it says 'he would run
me through at which time your deponent cried fire.'"

"Probably like a judge," Albert retorted. He was becoming frustrated with those who did not know what the words meant. When
Jessica insisted that a *cutlass* was a hat with "one of those big rims,"
he dismissed this description by emphatically saying, "A cutlass is a
type of sword and bayonets are a type of gun."

Other supervisors were not as interested in the words. Tom,
whose concerns were of a different bent, suggested cheekily that
William might actually be a woman. "Why does he claim that he has
a breast?" he asked. Gleeful laughter from the group ensued. Even
Selene battered a smile. "Boys don't have breasts," he continued.
"Boys have chests, not breasts!" Albert was overcome with laughter.
He bent over his desk, almost hysterical. Noticing the captive audience, Tom labored the point, "And why would a boy soldier make
a pass at another boy?" He was referring to William LeBaron's

observation that a soldier came up to him, "damned" him, and "made several passes" at him with a drawn sword, "the last of which the sword went between [his] arm and breast."

In my early days of teaching, I might have dismissed Tom's question, "Why does he claim that he has a breast?" as an attempt to undermine the work and my authority. However, I realized that not only was the document's particular English phrasing a legitimate source of interest, but the humor that Tom generated seemed to be liberating. What a contrast to the way we had begun our previous attempt at process drama! Beyond Tom's humor, however, the encounter demonstrates the complexity of learning and process drama. Note these observations:

- The students are physically creating a space in contrast to their normal learning environment. The teacher signals that something different will occur in this space. He doesn't tell them how to respond, but rather launches into a narrative about a mysterious document that has to be addressed by a group of supervisors. The group is caught up in a dramatic encounter, and the learning is geared into how they respond to it. The learning is taking place *in the process drama,* and students have to find meaning from within that encounter.
- The group must discover through their role what a document without a context could mean. They discuss particular phrasing and the definitions of words. Their role as supposed expert scholars generates much amusement as they begin to play with and imagine what the document, and the "important find," holds for them. The students are learning *through the process drama* something about a historical period; the drama aims at facilitating their growth in understanding.
- The leader is discovering that his aims for choosing this document, as they relate to the exploration of the liberty boys, will not be realized. The leader is reminded, as the students will be later, that this way of working often results in aims and objectives being renegotiated in the process. The leader is learning *about process drama* that it is difficult—virtually impossible—to predict how a group will respond to a lived event.

It seemed important to tap into what sense the group was making of the material. After submitting to the unfamiliarity of the language, the students, in role as supervisors, eagerly developed a list of questions they had about this strange remnant from the past:

What caused this fight?
Who is William LeBaron of Boston?
What was LeBaron doing in King Street?
Why were the soldiers so angry?
Why was the boy in distress?
What happened to William?
Why did the soldiers threaten William LeBaron?
Why did William LeBaron write this article?

When the group, back out of role, examined the supervisors' questions, their interest in the document became clearer. Meryl proposed that the supervisors' questions were focused on the man, William LeBaron. "They want to know why he testified," she exclaimed. "They want to know about this guy. They want to know things about him. His background." In her journal that evening she pursued this point, "What was he doing in King St. on March 5? Why did he testify? Is he telling the truth?" Albert reflects equally on LeBaron's honesty: "because then I will know if the testimony was likely to be true." In questioning LeBaron's motivations, probing beneath the words, and looking for hints of equivocation, Albert and Meryl were demonstrating a sophisticated social studies skill: They recognized that without knowing the contextual background to the details, an incomplete picture would remain.

Heathcote's (1976) plea for teachers to help children develop topics they are interested in spoke strongly to my structural thinking here. Having students formulate their own ideas and concerns, she says, is "the paste that holds the drama together" (121). Students are likely to have greater investment in the activity if they are the source of its construction. I needed to recognize what interest the LeBaron document created for the students. Superimposing my own agenda might have jeopardized their energy and excitement in the material. It seemed such a simple thing to ask them to examine their own questions, when students raise their own questions, they are beginning to take control over what interests them, and what is worth knowing. Questions prompt inquiry. Yet too often it is the teachers who are asking the questions and thereby controlling the power base.

It was becoming more apparent that if the students' questions were different from my own, then we would need to renegotiate the work. Students are not going to take interest in something foreign to them. As Graves (1982) says, "When people own a place they look after it. When it belongs to someone else, they couldn't care less" (Calkins 1982, 115). The process drama was allowing the students to be placed on the inside of their learning, and, from that perspective, it was permitting the group to control the boundaries of what it was they hoped to discover. Social studies educators echo these concerns. "Pupils' interest," Hanna (1987) argues, "must be aroused before pupil effort attends the lesson" (7). One way of arousing interest, Newmann (1988) suggests, is to invite the students to offer their own explanations and reasons for unfamiliar phenomena.

Simply put, process drama places the students on the inside so that they can be caught up within an artistic event (learning in), which helps them generate their own meanings (learning through), so that they can better direct, control, and submit to the encounter (learning about). This chapter and the next two will explore these different orientations more comprehensively.

LEARNING IN PROCESS DRAMA

"Many years ago," I narrated for my students, "William LeBaron saw things and participated in events that he was not pleased with. These events made a lasting impact on his conscience." Although we could have talked about what these "events" might have been, at my suggestion students prepared in three small groups a reenactment of one critical incident that made an impression upon William's psyche, an incident that revealed why he had a negative view of the soldiers. No further preparation was given, other than what the students already had read and discussed about the LeBaron testimony. This step, I thought, was a demanding one. We were now moving to an "acting out" mode.

Often, small-groups dramatizing, or *improvisation* as it is commonly called, is the task drama teachers most frequently begin with; yet if it is introduced too soon, it can lead to the groups' producing artificial and lackluster work. Heathcote, critical of those who demand this kind of "instant acting," argues that teachers must find ways of "protecting" students into drama so that they do not feel vulnerable or exposed.

Notions of "protection" and "acting out" were apparently not the contemplations of the students, however, as they eagerly set to the task of role-playing a key moment from LeBaron's life. As the three groups prepared to enact their scenes simultaneously, I planned to ask them occasionally to "freeze" the action and voice their thoughts. I assumed slowing down the action in this manner might build intensity. The groups eagerly went to their opening positions. I repeated the earlier narrative on the events William LeBaron witnessed years ago and how these might have shaped his psyche. The improvisations tentatively began. Every few seconds, the action would be "frozen."

"They're such a nice couple," Susan said, in role as LeBaron's mother, while watching Tom, as William, and Selene, as his wife, going off to the market. Mrs. LeBaron was unaware that her son was in imminent danger: Around a corner a soldier was waiting for William with a whip. Teddy, looking more comfortable in this grouping than in his grouping for the education tableau, voiced the soldier's thought, "I'm going to get a crack out of this." Soon he would bring havoc into a moment of domestic bliss. "This is fun!" the soldier later declared as he mercilessly beat William. As William's wife, Selene cried and watched her husband fall, "We need more help," but time was not on the victim's side. As his last breath was taken from him, William murmured, "I see my life passing before me."

In another group, Jessica, in role as a soldier, peered through LeBaron's kitchen window. As she watched the family, consisting of Albert, Madelene, and Amara, eating, she thought, "They better give me a place to stay and some food." Those words contrasted with Albert's contemplations as William, "It's a nice homely feeling here." Later in that scene, Jessica would storm into the kitchen and, in a moment of terror, seize an infant. "My baby!" Madelene moaned, seeing her child thrown on the floor.

I watched with interest as the soldiers were consistently being painted as villainous thugs, intent on bringing despair and unhappiness into LeBaron's home. Even in the third group, Brenda, as the soldier, said, "I'm going to get more soldiers and get you guys," after a brawl on a street with LeBaron (Joyce) and a youth (Meryl). Even though this scene, like Jessica's, hinted that the soldiers were provoked, this was not a dominant theme.

What I did read as pronounced in the groups' work was a tension between two opposing forces, harmony and chaos. There was,

I felt, something inherently dramatic in this: William as unknowing victim, and soldier as cunning terrorist. As I watched the work, it appeared that the moments that were the most demanding for the students to hold were when those two forces met: Teddy whipping Tom, Jessica throwing the baby on the floor, Brenda being beaten. It was these moments that generated the most amusement for the group, often leading to the students' momentarily breaking out of the drama by laughing. What appeared less demanding, and, iron-ically, more interesting, was the build up in the tension: Jessica stalking outside the LeBaron home and Teddy waiting for his vic-tim. If drama, as Beckerman (1970) maintains, "yearns forward, moves, evolves, is always in a state of becoming" (148), it was this element that arrested me as a watcher; I wondered whether it would captivate the class.

When the scenes were shared, the spectators were endowed with various roles. These roles were determined by the students; they were now framing the action. Susan's group asked the watchers to imagine they were neighbors who had heard about the incident at the market; Brenda's group thought the audience might have directly witnessed their scene from being on the street when it occurred; and Albert's group suggested that the spectators proba-bly had been told a rumor of what happened in LeBaron's kitchen.

I was hoping that if the audience members were, in a sense, par-ticipants in the action, this engagement would help emphasize con-tent over performance. It was important that those watching would not become passive spectators criticizing a theatrical performance. How effectively the students were in creating their roles was not an aim of this activity; the focus was on the information that the stu-dents were communicating about LeBaron. If the spectators were on the "inside" of the experience, they might respect and build belief in it more. This notion of reflecting in the process drama rather than outside of it would become a central feature of the work in later episodes.

When the scenes were shared, some students included props. Madelene, for example, had a toy baby; Jessica was wearing what resembled a soldier's hat; and Teddy grabbed a yardstick for his whip. These props seemed to help focus the attention of all partic-ipants. At the conclusion of each moment, I wandered up to the "watchers" and asked what they thought about the rumors circulat-ing around Boston. "Did you hear," I began, "what happened in LeBaron's house?"

"A soldier," replied Susan, "came in and tried to beat up William and tried to hurt the baby."

I nodded in sympathy, "I heard that too. How's the baby?"

"Brain-dead," added Teddy.

"I wonder," I continued, "when all this hardship is coming to an end?"

For that evening's journal assignment, we decided that letter writing might be something colonists would do. The group seemed to embrace their role as active spectators as they wrote as Bostonians to distant relatives or acquaintances. Madelene asks, after telling of the increased violence in Boston, "Do you think the soldiers will come back for revenge?" Albert reflects on the seething brutality, "I have a feeling this town won't be the same again." Amara, writing a poignant letter to an imaginary friend, was concerned about her own immediate physical welfare:

Dear Maggie:

Long time no see, how are you doing now in Virginia? Now in Boston up here, it's not that good. Soldiers are going around demanding and hurting my friends, neighborhoods, and all people in Boston who doesn't have power. Just yesterday morning on the street I saw a soldier beating up a man for no reason, he just felt like it and we patriots can do nothing about it. That's why now life in Boston is very hard if you are a patriot. Is Virginia like that too, or is it better?

I'm very scared and afraid now that maybe the soldier will soon get to my house. Last night my next door neighbor have been hurted already. A soldier went in their house and slapped the daughter, hurted the son and even threw a 2-month old baby on the floor. I'm really scared now and hope that the soldiers would stop it. Hope Virginia isn't like that. Write back and tell me about it.

Your friend,
Amara

Boston was beginning to take a concrete shape for the group, and that shape seemed layered with tension. There were the powerful and the powerless, the safe and the not so safe, the violent and the timid. With an uncanny intuitivelike sense, the group was suggesting that what was drawing them into our imagined world were these moments of contrast, and particularly how these contrasts might be resolved. Although elements of this world had been teacher-structured (for instance, the convention of being able to hear someone's thoughts had a dramatic quality that I deliberately folded in), the opportunities provided for student-structuring strengthened and generated belief in our improvised play.

It appeared, for example, that when the students decided upon the spectators' roles by suggesting that one scene was a "rumor," this strategy provided yet another color to our picture of Boston. Boston was a city where eavesdropping and spying seemed part of daily life. Furthermore, although William LeBaron was initially the catalyst for the groups as they formulated the scenes, the students' writing focused less on the man and more on the milieu, and particularly on their own attitude to that milieu. "I heard rumors about soldiers beating up on people," Jessica wrote. "I don't know how true it is, but I wouldn't put anything past those sneaky little excuses for humans. If that is true, all of the people have decided to go after them, including me. So I was wondering if you guys would mind coming here and joining us." There was an agenda coming through their writing. It had less of a "teacher imposed" quality, and it was reading more like a natural outgrowth of the classwork.

Yet the writing also pointed toward a possible and mysterious future. What was going to happen if the violence increased? How would individuals respond if it did? Were there others who might help? What means did we have of verifying the rumors? I was struck by the ominous foreboding in their words, by their pervasive concern with destiny. Drama, Langer (1953) has argued, deals essentially with future commitments, and persons in drama are "makers of the future." There was a sense that the group was starting to forge their own futures in the unfolding dramatic encounter.

Learning in process drama is then characterized by what happens to a group when they are caught in the process of art making. There is a quality to the reflection or contemplation taking place within a process drama that is quite different from when the group steps out of the process drama. This quality has something to do with permitting yourself to be open to the possible worlds that artworks yield, an ability to release yourself to the role-play and allow the experience to massage your senses. This release does not necessarily mean that students are engaged in extensive dramatic playing sessions. We can see that one feature of the work to date is that the commitment to belief occurs through a shifting frame of reference, in which the students are constantly encouraged to look at the same events through different eyes—through their development, as it were, of multiple viewpoints through the enactment of various roles.

Learning in drama highlights the process of being caught up in events and being challenged to respond to them in the moment at which they are occurring. In many respects, the quality of learning available to students when they submit to the process of making and creating drama honors the nature of the artistic medium itself. Just as when we watch a good play and are arrested by the events as they affect the characters' lives, in process drama it is *the experience of being caught up in* that forces us to have a reaction. We must not deny the power of participation in drama itself. Many teachers seem more concerned in the learning that happens after the drama, or that which can be recounted or quantified at a lesson's close, but to focus on such learning as the principal method of how the form operates misrepresents the dramatic medium.

Judith McLean (1996), an Australian, has recently written on the nature of the aesthetic event in the classroom. She found that learning in drama seems very much glued to developing within students what some have referred to as an aesthetic framework. For instance, my students' hunch that Boston was rife with power plays of one kind or another seemed of sufficient interest that we could now further explore some of the issues raised by the Boston Massacre, particularly the growing disquiet in the relationship between the patriotic and colonial forces. In searching for a role context through which this exploration could continue, I recalled Heathcote's formative essay, "Signs and Portents" (1984b), which argued that groups in drama sometimes can reflect more closely on events if they are "asked to comment on the action" rather than directly participate in it "at life-rate" (168). O'Neill (1988) elaborates on this position:

> Where involvement in the action predominates, the reflective element is necessarily weakened. With too intense an involvement, the sense of control which is so important a part of the spectator's pleasure in theatre and drama, is weakened. A truly engaged yet detached aesthetic response is in fact more demanding than total involvement. (15)

Learning in process drama can then be facilitated by the selecting of a stance or viewpoint that helps participants develop an aesthetic response to the material being created. The aesthetic response can be supported by finding a role or position through which the students can make decisions about judgment and value.

The viewpoint of a time traveler, for instance, suggested itself to me as a possible frame by which my students could reflect on Boston. Not only did it link with the "People of the Future" role, but it also neatly appealed as a "distancing" frame through which the group could begin to "ask questions, weigh evidence, investigate events, make judgments, reach decisions and draw conclusions" (O'Neill 1988, 15).

When the students were invited to close their eyes and imagine that they were entering a time capsule that took them back to eighteenth-century Boston, their first impressions of the city as the capsule door opened were noticeably vivid. "What do you see?" I asked of the students as they sat at their tables, arms folded, heads rested, eyes closed.

NADIA: Horses and carriages.

TEDDY: Waste products made by horses on the floor.

SUSAN: Horse-drawn carriages with people.

PHIL: And what are the people doing?

SUSAN: They're walking around and some are in the carriages.

PHIL: And the streets? What are they like?

SUSAN: They're dusty and unpaved paths . . . and people are walking and talking to their neighbors.

MADELENE: Women wearing beautiful dresses holding umbrellas.

PHIL: I wonder where they're going?

MADELENE: Maybe shopping.

PHIL: Showing off their fine clothes. Walking through the streets.

JOYCE: I see robbers and soldiers having a gunfight.

PHIL: Violence on the streets.

BRENDA: Women wearing hoop skirts . . . Walking around the streets.

ALBERT: Dogs smelling and barking at everyone.

PHIL: Frightened of those dogs?

ALBERT: No.

AMARA: Drunkards walking around . . .

SELENE: People buying things . . .

TOM: Soldiers on horses rushing into the village.

PHIL: I wonder why they're in a hurry?

JESSICA: Dirt roads and trees.

MERYL: I see a duel between two people. I think they're cowboys.

They had imagined a virtual Georgian landscape where wealth and decadence contrasted with violence and poverty. At one impromptu moment, Jessica and Nadia offered the sounds of dogs barking as a soundtrack while others shared their images. Their historically appropriate vision excited me, particularly when I considered that the only formal reading we had engaged in to this point was LeBaron's document. Perhaps some of their impressions had been gleaned from movies or television, or from other reading matter.

Here we see how the process of looking from the inside out had enabled the students to create a fictitious landscape that perhaps weeks of reading would not have done. Their aesthetic response developed from the position(s) or stances that they were invited to enter. Interestingly, the activity itself generated considerable interest from the class. Nadia's insight that it is "easy for you to picture something with your eyes closed" struck a chord with others. The students' imaginations were richly descriptive yet, as Albert reminded us in his writing, they had rarely been tapped: "Most teachers want students to sit up straight and be attentive. Heads down shows that we're tire and teachers usually makes us sit up!" What are schools doing to our children? Given that this school had seemingly thwarted their creative impulses, it was comforting that they were still able to enter into the dramatic activities.

It is this ironic quality of being both a participant and a spectator in process drama that seems to assist in both the development of a range of different viewpoints and an aesthetic response. O'Neill (1991b) argues that teachers should aim not to limit students' perspectives by entrapping them within a single role. "We need to promote a more active frame of mind in our students," she proposes, one that permits the development of the "kinds of perspective on the work which will allow them to operate in a way that is both involved and detached, sympathetic and scientific" (141). I find much sense in this idea. Learning in drama then is generated by frames that encourage a dialogue between being both participant and spectator.

When the seventh graders were role-playing a critical incident in LeBaron's life, then later assuming the roles of those who might have witnessed that event, they appeared to be looking in and out, using role as "microscope and searchlight" (O'Neill 1991b, 41). Later, when envisaging in more general terms the character of the town of Boston, a further role detachment was layered in, which seemed to shape yet another impression. This promotion of a multiplicity of perspectives has also been suggested as a primary function of the social studies teacher (see Jarolimek 1977). Carpenter (1969), for example, argued that social studies teachers must assist their students to become "active thinkers" (154). An active thinker is defined as one "seeking, probing, processing data from [the] environment towards a variety of destinations" best suited to individual "mental characteristics." It seemed that when the seventh-grade students devised their own questions on the document, developed possible incidents that led to LeBaron's writing it, and shared and then contemplated each of these moments, they were approaching the curriculum in an active and thoughtful manner. If teachers are able to encourage such a climate when they begin a new topic, perhaps their students will respond to social studies with greater interest and commitment.

Beyond the multiple perspectives that reflecting in role provides, another aspect to learning in process drama is the questions that students begin to ask about the social studies concepts being explored. "I don't think I have enough information to tell if the soldiers were at fault," Albert reflected in his journal, which led to his searching out a children's book entitled *The Story of the Boston Massacre* (Phelan 1976). Tom was intrigued with the various battles of the revolution and brought to class a collection of drawings and sketches contained in *Voices from America's Past,* whereas Susan and Madelene were more interested in the historical figures of Patrick Henry and Benedict Arnold, respectively. I encouraged the students to read widely around the period. "Do we have to do book reports on these like we do in Reading?" Teddy asked. He was referring to the subject that all students took. Teddy seemed surprised when we spent some time sharing these materials, flicking through pages, and listening to the researchers elaborate on any discoveries they might have uncovered. Nadia, Jessica, and Meryl were the only ones who had not completed research.

Selene and Teddy were surprised to discover that they had the same book, *The American Revolution,* although their texts had different cover designs. "That picture is called *The Spirit of '76*," Tom said of Teddy's book, "and I think [Selene's cover] is when George Washington and his soldiers were crossing the Delaware after fighting the British." A lively discussion ensued on what *Spirit* referred to. "Those soldiers," asserted Nadia, referring to Washington's troops, "are ready for whoever comes." Albert declared, "It was glorious before the war," as he contemplated what "Spirit of 76" might have implied.

In the Piagetian model, Calkins (1982) argues, growth does not happen in a vacuum: "Organisms . . . grow in response to interactions which challenge them, interactions which dislodge one equilibrium so that a new one can be reached" (221). Parker (1991) agrees. "Analyzing, interpreting and manipulating" data in the social studies classroom, he urges, are vital for intellectual development (6). But in our work these interactions or learnings were being supported by the kind of reflecting students were able to commit to in the drama.

Learning in process drama demands that leaders and participants can:

- honor the fundamental nature of a dramatic encounter and seek meaning from within the medium
- reflect from inside the drama or reflect in the action
- operate as both spectator and participant
- permit the experience of engagement and detachment to work upon their senses so that participants can both submit and control
- establish multiple perspectives that support an aesthetic response

One of the many demands of learning in process drama is the necessity for participants to "think from within a dilemma instead of talking coolly about the dilemma" (Heathcote 1976, 118). Heathcote reminds us that this dilemma is particularized within a given imaginary time and place. The situation in which the drama occurs, she argues, needs to be clearly focused, and the tasks participants engage in need to be concrete. These decisions are often determined in relation to the subject being explored. For example, when working with a class of fifteen-year-olds on the topic "Loyalty in Tudor England," Heathcote (1976) considered the following issues:

> How do I introduce the whole idea of loyalty? What strategy will I
> use whereby there shall be a slow realization that the choices
> between loyalty and disloyalty become available to the class? And,
> how do I do this within a Tudor framework? And what shall be
> the dilemma? What will make it possible for them to make
> that choice? (118)

Her goal through this planning stage was to uncover ultimately a specific moment in time that would endow the students with particular roles and actions. The dilemma or choices that the group might later face might emerge from these roles and actions. Heathcote warns that once students are faced with a dilemma, teachers should avoid deciding what choices students will make. The decisions students take and the kind of conceptual learning that is possible through process drama is the subject of the next chapter.

3

Shifting Perspectives
Learning Through
Process Drama

It would be fair to say that a dominating concern of process drama is its orientation toward challenging participants' perspectives and having participants become accountable for any stance or viewpoint that they might assume in the drama. Changes in understanding are not always easy to demonstrate, however, and, as some critics of process drama have asserted, are impossible to prove. But the leader in process drama is consciously working toward transforming perspectives and exploring human experience.

Reflection, understanding, and *knowledge generation* are terms we associate with what is happening to participants in a process drama. These were certainly at the core of Dorothy Heathcote's practice, as Muir (1996) reminds us:

> It is through the awakening of what Heathcote terms the 'self-spectator', which is the participants being aware of what they are doing while they are doing it, that she aims to bring about knowledge and change. It is with this key concept of the self-spectator that the objectives of knowledge and change coincide, because what is being created is not simply knowing something but knowing how you have come to know it through what you have done. (25–26)

Heathcote is concerned with having her students operate at a meta-cognitive level in which they see their own actions being played out in front of them. Learning through process drama implies that participants are being challenged to face and confront their own actions, and the task for the leader is to find situations in which these challenges can be met.

Learning through process drama demands that leaders and participants can:

- acknowledge that students generate meanings for themselves in and on action
- hold up positions so that they can be revealed and interrogated
- incorporate an array of strategies (e.g., small-group work, writing in and on role, and teacher-in-role) that help participants confront the work's themes
- recognize that process drama is concerned with shifts in thinking and changes in understanding
- honor the significance that the art form has in the lifelong learning of the group
- understand the nexus between art and learning.

In my process drama, the time had come, I believed, to find a dilemma that Boston patriots could face that in turn might help the students understand something about themselves and the period we were studying. Although my seventh graders appeared interested in the events of the Boston Massacre, they were not being challenged to confront some of the dilemmas faced by the views represented by LeBaron. More than twenty years ago, Heathcote (1971) boldly claimed:

> I want my classes to learn to make decisions, and to understand the problems and rewards of these decisions, so I regard it as my prime task to ensure that they clearly understand the choice between possibilities, the nature of the decision taken and the demands likely to be put upon them because of the decision taken. This is another reason why drama is such a wonderful educational tool. (48)

She was espousing a view of teaching and learning that would later support Eisner's (1981) outlook that the arts can be cognitive activities "that make unique forms of meaning possible" (48). I concluded that the time had come to see what position(s) my students would develop, and possibly defend, if they once again found themselves as participants in the society of revolutionary Boston. What "unique forms of meaning" might be illuminated? What might they learn through the process drama when encountered with some oppositional force?

DRAMATIC FOCUS

In our drama, I wanted to help the group face "real" dilemmas. The challenge was not only for me to find a dilemma of sufficient interest to the students, but also for me to find one that might have resonated during the Boston Massacre. In the previous chapter, I discussed how the society of pre-Revolutionary Boston was taking shape in our classroom, and described how the learning was supported by the art form itself. As I reflected upon the tensions evident in the students' perceptions of eighteenth-century Boston, I considered the possible dilemmas that might be worth exploring. Colonists at that time appeared to be concerned with what their economic future entailed in light of the taxes placed on them by the British. What happened to colonists who protested British occupation? What stresses might they have encountered? Our work on LeBaron had indicated rival factions between the colonial and patriotic forces. What lengths might patriots be prepared to go to support their cause? The Boston landscape was potentially rich in dramatic material because it was layered with tension. However, it did not suggest to me an immediate situation in which the students might encounter an interesting dilemma and thereby begin to learn through the dramatic art form something about themselves and the world in which they lived.

Drama, Byron (1986) notes, "cannot function at the level of generalities, it requires a very specific setting in time, place and action" (44). Although narrowing a particular focus for our drama on the Boston Massacre was initially difficult, I was once again helped by the students, in this case by the historical research they had embarked on. For instance, as I scanned the opening pages of Albert's library book, (Phelan 1976), there seemed to be possible approaches to my structural concerns about dramatic focus.

The book opened with the plans of influential patriot leaders, such as Sam and John Adams, Paul Revere, and William Molineux, who had just learned that ten thousand British soldiers were about to enter Boston Harbor. A secret patriots' meeting was being arranged where the "Whig" sympathizers could discuss the growing "Tory" menace. I followed a hunch and decided to read some sections of the book aloud to the class as a pretext to dramatic activity.

The students were seated on the floor grouped in front of me. "Sam Adams," I read, "slips from the group at the Bunch of Grapes tavern beckoning his fellow patriot Will Molineux to follow him." I attempted to shroud my reading by coloring it with an atmosphere of urgency and mystery. "Once outside the taproom," I continued in a lowered voice, "Adams whispers that the news [of the soldiers' arrival] is not unexpected, still their closest associates should be alerted. There are decisions to be made this very night. Molineux is in agreement and offers his home as a meeting place." After a moment's pause, I asked the class to think of a message that Adams might have sent to his patriot friends. "Secretly pass your message on to somebody else by whispering it into your neighbor's ear." The room was busy with the networking of messages. The students' interest seemed baited.

"If you were going to attend William Molineux's house that night," I interjected before the networking ceased, "what route do you think you would take in Boston?"

NADIA: I would go through little alleys where no one could see me. . . . With something covering my face.

PHIL: Yes . . . no one could see you.

TOM: Once in a while look to see if anyone was following you.

PHIL: I wonder why you wouldn't want anyone to know where you were going?

NADIA: Because if one of the soldiers saw that you were going there they would get suspicious and tell all the rest of the soldiers and then they'd attack you.

PHIL: You would be in fear.

JESSICA: Well if it wasn't a soldier . . . and just a person and they said "Where are you going?" . . . and they might be like undercover . . . and so attack.

PHIL: So to be a patriot in those days it must have been . . .

NADIA: Sneaky!

MERYL: Dangerous.

PHIL: Some risk involved in being a patriot.

TOM: And you would want to know how to keep a secret.

PHIL (Contemplatively): You would need to know how to keep a secret. . . . Would you like to reconstruct what it might have been like to be a patriot attending that meeting?

Their reading of the text suggested a "cloak and dagger" quality in a patriot's life; they had focused on the risks involved. Not only would a patriot have to exercise caution walking through the streets of Boston, but he or she would also need to be trustworthy and courageous. Quite subtly, I was hoping to endow the students with the role of patriots who might have attended that meeting at Molineux's. In structuring, however, it seemed appropriate to strengthen some of the stressful characteristics the group was suggesting of the patriots' journey to Molineux's house. I decided that an effective way of structuring the activity might be to play a reworking of the game "Hunted and Hunter" (Booth 1986). We would call our version "Tory and Whig."

In this game, two players are blindfolded, one is called the hunter (in our version, the Tory), the other is called the hunted (the Whig). The other participants stand and create a circle with the two players in the center. The object of the game is for the hunter/Tory to catch the hunted/Whig. The others prevent or assist the players to achieve their respective goal. To avoid injury, the players walk in the circle with their arms folded.

I was unprepared for the near hysteria that this game initially provoked. It almost seemed cathartic for the spectators as they stood in a circle and watched the tentative steps of the two blindfolded volunteers adopt a cat-and-mouse strategy as one tried to escape the clutches of the other. "Man, what a fabulous day," Albert wrote in his journal that evening, while reflecting on his own enthusiastic attempts as the Tory searching out for the evasive Whig, in this instance Susan. "I try to advoid using my hands, seeing the accidents Teddy had on Jessica, but it was too hard and I keep banging into them. It was very fun," he went on. "School needs live action."

Bolton (1984) has written on the power of game as a tension-building device in drama. Although I was working for this effect, it was a challenge to put the game in a context in which the students could generate information that might be helpful in our forthcoming patriots' meeting. "The Whig must get to the meeting undetected," I reminded the class as Nadia was being blindfolded. "The Tory must catch the Whig." In this instance, the blindfolded Tom frantically waved his arms around at the Whig while he frequently bumped into those standing nearby. It was difficult to prevent the spectators from submitting totally to the game element. My structuring in previous activities had indicated, however, that if I invited the spectators to imagine they were participants in the action, it would support the lens through which they saw and thereby respond to the activity.

I suggested that those observing could narrate the journey of the Whig and the Tory on this particular evening. "There was a Whig walking around," Teddy began, in good humor, while commenting on Nadia's aimless moves.

"She heard," Meryl suggested, "that the Tories knew about this meeting."

Watching the action of the protagonist and antagonist seemed to help the observers construct a narrative. Brenda continued, noticing Nadia's quick maneuver at changing direction: "The Whig tries to move through the streets without being seen."

"On the other hand the Tory," said Susan, "tried to find out where they are going and what sort of meeting they are going to have."

"Because," interrupted Joyce, "some Whigs talk to him rudely." This subtle shift of spectator focus seemed to transform the game from a singularly "fun" activity to one in which we had ownership of the story.

"We all have our own unique stories," Barton and Booth (1990) tell us, "our own ways of storying, our own ways of representing what is, what was, and what might be" (14). By inviting, coaxing, and, in some instances, cajoling the class members to share aspects of their story of a Boston journey many years ago, I was hoping to help them become participants in the action.

I noted with particular interest in my log how exciting it was when Tom, as the blindfolded Tory, finally "caught" and then confronted the Whig:

He immediately questioned her on her movements. "Where are you going?" he demanded. "Home," Nadia hesitantly responded. Undeterred the Tory persisted, "What are you doing out at this time of night?" "I'm just going for a walk." "Well," Tom retorted, "you're looking very suspicious as you are walking backwards . . . and looking over your shoulder."

What was wonderful about this exchange was the manner in which the game seemed to have naturally strengthened and built the patriots' experience that evening. The power of narrating yourself and others in the action seems a useful strategy for developing the necessary distance in order to reflect on the work.

The game had supported the "state of tension" often considered important in process drama (Bolton 1984, 88).

Before we set out to attend the Molineux meeting I contemplated what the students could create or possess that would help them individually view themselves as participants in the action. How might each identify with a patriot who had to decide on a strategy for thwarting the growing British presence? Playing the game was an important step in generating group interest, but I still felt that important background information was lacking. Other than the physical journey through the streets, what kinds of personal journeys had the patriots been on before this meeting? What might it have been like to have been a patriot in Boston during the eighteenth century?

I toyed with the idea of inviting group members to each compile a patriot's portrait, but I saw flaws with this approach. "Developing complicated characterizations," I mused, "could burden the students' role taking rather than empower it." I remembered how when I first began teaching drama I usually worked off the assumption that students needed to spend time preparing or rehearsing their roles before they could do anything "important." In my earlier years of teaching I had been especially influenced by Brian Way's *Development Through Drama* (1967), which focused on an exercise approach to classroom drama and the acquisition of so-called life skills. It has only been in recent years that I have deliberately structured so that participants can create their roles during the work. This change has largely developed from Bolton's (1979) criticism of those who emphasize "training children in their drama to imitate," which can inhibit participants from responding naturally. Furthermore, I have been influenced by Heathcote's (1980b) belief that students can sometimes stake out a personal claim in the realm of exploration by possibly creating an object or drawing a picture related to the theme. Such can sometimes assist an individual's commitment to the drama.

As I reflected upon the patriots' journey through the streets of Boston, I wondered whether they might have encountered the risk-taking hazards that our Whigs faced. I studied a map of Boston drawn in 1770 (Figure 3–1) and wondered what it must have been like being a patriot working at the Granary on Treamont Street or the ropewalks on Cow Lane. What might the quality of life have been on Belcher's Lane or Milk Street? Did the patriots congregate in certain areas of the town? I also wondered about the patriots' expectations of the Molineux meeting. Would they all agree to one approach to take with the British? The map was helping me construct possible narratives. I hoped it might serve the function of having the students stake out a personal claim.

On a long white strip of paper, we had drawn an enormous map of Boston in 1770. This map was then attached to the wall. The students were standing in front of the map surveying Boston's topography when I posed the question, "Where do you think William Molineux lives?" They looked at the places of interest we had marked on the map. "On the lower end of Marlborough Street," Nadia suggested, "by the Liberty Tree." The students seemed to like the idea that Molineux would live near the Liberty Tree. Nadia then wrote an *X* on the map to indicate Molineux's house.

"Now," I proceeded, "if we are going to attend this meeting at Molineux's, we have to get there first." Using different colored markers, each student then located a place on the map where he or she lived. As they were contemplating and recording possibilities, I noted some of the patriots' abodes. An outline of the map the group drew is reconstructed in Figure 3–2. "Nadia lives on Lynn Street," I observed. "Jessica lives over on North Square. Joyce in front of the Old State House. Susan over near Faneuil Hall, and Meryl seems to be on Sunbury Street." Some patriots were changing their minds about where they lived. "But I moved," Meryl retorted. "I now live on North Street." They seemed to be enjoying discussing the various street names and noting the different sites.

"In your own color," I suggested, "draw the route you took on that dark and lonely night to Molineux's house." With a hive of activity, the group excitedly applied marker to paper. Some took complicated routes. "You come up here," I said to Tom, pointing

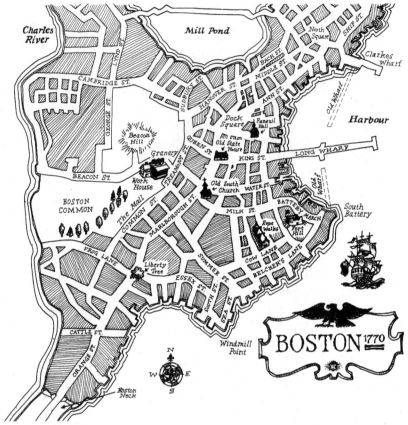

FIGURE 3–1   *Map of 1770 Boston*

to where he had drawn many circles around Boston Common, "I wonder why?"

"I was playing tag," he offered. "It was early."

"Would you be playing tag," I challenged him, "if you are going to this meeting?"

"But it was pretty early," he persisted. Albert and Teddy started to laugh. They had drawn more direct routes. "It was five or six o'clock," Tom went on. "I decided to go around this tree. Then I sort of joked around. And then I went to Clarke's Wharf and swam in the harbor, and finally onto Long Wharf."

Although I thought that Tom had defied the logic of the patriots' quick taproom exit to meet at Molineux's, I let his explanation pass with the suggestion that perhaps he was one of the liberty boys

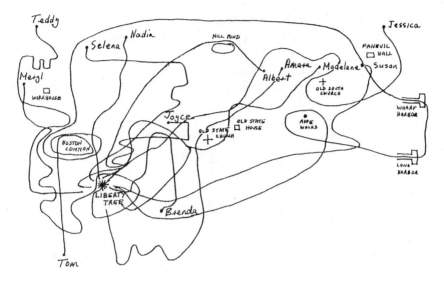

FIGURE 3–2   *Reconstructed student map of the patriots' route*

"who caused some of the trouble" in Boston. I believed that my structuring was flawed in that we had not reminded ourselves of the meeting's contexts, particularly the patriots' desire to assemble immediately and discuss appropriate plans given the arrival of the soldiers. However, I later regretted not questioning Tom more on the kind of patriot he might have been. As Duckworth (1987) argues, "the right question at the right time can move children to peaks in their thinking that result in significant steps forward and real intellectual excitement" (5).

Back at the map, I noticed that Amara had drawn a route that looked like a cardiogram just before arriving at the Liberty Tree. "Those are alleys," she quietly said noticing my interest. "I went back around my steps through the alleys."

"She doesn't want anyone to follow her," Teddy added.

Most of the journeys had now been drawn "You are all taking different routes," I observed.

We then surveyed the map for interesting patterns. "Most people live on the westside," Teddy argued.

"We live in groups," retorted Tom.

"Except for Joyce," I noticed, "who is located roughly in the center of town all by herself. Where might her loyalties lie?" There seemed to be a contemplative pause after I raised that question.

The landscape was being filtered with potential stories. Neighbors were located and places of interest discussed. "It is all very relaxing and peaceful," Albert later wrote of his neighborhood, "but sometimes the British soldiers come around and we would all be very quiet and look mean and menacing." Menacing seemed to describe aptly the journeys that the patriots took that evening. "I realized that someone was following, so I walked faster to Cow Lane," Amara wrote in her journal, "and I looked back and saw a shadow. . . . It was only a cat." Other patriots' journeys were dangerous too. "It was cold and dreary," echoed Nadia. "I left the house, clenching my penguin pass . . . I used a different route to get there, taking allies and underground passes." *Penguin* was a password that the group thought the patriots might use to enter Molineux's.

Brenda's journal entry was particularly evocative: "Not even a mouse was stirring. I felt strong heavy winds blowing in my face as I was plodding through the snow." I felt her writing was characterized by a greater sense of purpose than her previous entries. She described the difficulties faced in safely arriving at Molineux's. "When I finally reached to Frog Lane I turned East to the Liberty Tree. But that's not it. I still have to circle the entire block to try to confuse the person who is following me."

Their interest in mystery and secrecy led me to suggest that the patriots' meeting always starts with an oath. "Like an expression of loyalty," Albert added. "Or a group promise," noted Nadia. The swearing of an oath might indicate aspects of the patriots' life that we would shortly assume. Oaths can also serve a ritualistic function: They unite and bind (Scheff 1979). They can also make demands. Heathcote has often drawn on the power of ritual to create group solidarity (Wagner 1976; Heathcote and Bolton 1995). In this instance, I surmised that if the patriots had a contract with one another it might be fruitful to note the compromises, if any, they might face in living up to it. My structural thinking was to build commitment to the patriots' cause and then examine the costs of that commitment.

While the groups were busily preparing their oaths, I considered in my log the possibilities in which those oaths might be shared:

> I am thinking that it might be useful to prepare an alleyway that the patriots can weave around before entering Molineux's house. Alleys have come up frequently in their accounts so far. I asked

Teddy, Amara, and Albert if they could move to another part of the room while I put the desks in a cluttered arrangement: The patriots would have to move through these. Teddy asked whether "The penguin GAWKS at midnight" was a good oath. I concur that it is. I noticed that Tom appeared despondent at having to work with Brenda and Joyce. Poor Tom! He was dissatisfied with their oath "Patriots R Loyal." While I was hastily carving an alleyway with desks and tables listening to the groups as they frequently used words like "promise" and "loyal" in their oaths, it dawned on me that if I was to assume the role of someone other than Molineux at the meeting, an unexpected and unknown host, this possibly contains the seeds of dramatic interest, and might interestingly pose a dilemma for the patriots. How loyal would the patriots be to Molineux in his absence? How might they react to a stranger whose loyalties aren't immediately clear?

This log entry was characteristic of my improvised planning here. In this instance, I was spontaneously responding to the student preparations by shaping a physical space, hoping that this might be a useful scaffold for them to share their oaths. At the same time, I was searching for a dilemma that related to the oath's implicit assumptions. Listening to the students' planning helped. For example, if patriots are loyal, as Tom's group decided, how might they deal with a disloyal patriot? Assuming the role of a stand-in for Molineux appealed to me, for it would be the last thing, I surmised, the group was expecting. It constituted, in Bruner's (1962) language, an "effective surprise," and might therefore promote an interesting challenge.

"You won't recognize who I am!" I mentioned to the four groups of patriots as they were preparing to make their way down the alley. "I will open the door and let you into Molineux's house. You need to decide how you are going to walk down the alley and the manner in which you'll share your oath." Albert asked if the lights could be turned off to further create an atmospheric effect. While he shut off the lights, the other students arranged themselves at the end of the "alley," preparing to take the last few steps of their journey. I now hoped the groups had developed their own contexts for the meeting. They had played a game, drawn a route, written a journal entry of the journey from their home to the Liberty Tree, and created an oath.

"The patriots made their way to William Molineux's house," I began to narrate. Teddy, Albert, and Amara were the first to negotiate carefully a path through the desks. "Their journey to the Liberty Tree," I continued, "had been long and difficult." Albert was deviously clutching what looked like a weapon, while constantly looking over his shoulder. Teddy had drawn a sign, "No Lobsterbacks," which he held in front of his chest. As they arrived at the door, Amara, holding a toy penguin, knocked three times. The stranger opened it. "The Penguin," whispered Amara holding up the animal, "GAWKS" continued Teddy, "at midnight" completed Albert, while Amara furtively tapped the penguin on Albert's rifle three times. It was richly theatrical, aptly conveying aspects of the underworld which they felt the patriots inhabited. It seemed that for this group, at least, the previous steps were a useful precursor to the meeting.

"Were you seen by anyone?" I said, building belief in the foreboding picture they had created. "No," whispered Amara, looking a trifle uncertainly at the questioner. Soon the other patriots began their journey down the path. "We saw a Tory by the way," cried Jessica to the stranger at the door. "But he didn't see us!" The stranger seemed relieved. "We have our oath," Meryl offered. I raised my eyebrows, beckoning them to say it:

> *We the Boston Patriots*
> *Promise to say not*
> *The things we hear tonight*
> *At 7 on the dot*
> *If a soldier threaten us*
> *We won't reveal the plot*
> *So if we do*
> *God help us we shall ROT*

Unlike "The penguin GAWKS at midnight," this oath was said quite energetically. This vigorous recital created a more public feel to the meeting than the secretive tones the group had earlier suggested during the game and mapmaking. When all the patriots had entered, each oath was shared again.

I noticed that it was nearly 11:00 A.M. so this particular class session was about to end. The patriots commenced to discuss where Will was. Meryl suggested that Molineux might have been at the ropewalks, which seemed implausible to the others given the urgency of the meeting. "He might have been followed," suggested Teddy. If this was so, Molineux could have decided to seek protection at the ropewalks, thought Albert. As the patriots considered whether they should go and look for their host, I offered a narrative: "So the patriots were left having to decide what they were going to do in light of Molineux's absence. . . . And who was this unknown person hosting the meeting?" At this moment, the session ended. There was much excitement as the students grabbed their books and headed off to their next class. "What a mystery!" Tom said while opening the door.

The students' journal writing that evening constituted some of the most engaging entries I had read. Albert began with some observations on the oaths:

> Today we were to go through an alleyway and at the end was the house of the meeting. I was carrying an umbrella and pretending it to be a gun and I gave it to Teddy who slipped his sign over it and Amara knocked her penguin on it three times . . . Jessica and Meryl's code was in my opinion, pretty ridicuous considering the situation that all was to be quiet and mysterious. They did it like they were performing on stage as entertainment. They waved their hand all around. For some reason, they reminded me of a commercial of Broadway where all these girls were waving their legs up and waving their hands all around and light was flashing all over, streaking them with bright light.

His observations on the girls' oath were illuminating in that it suggested Albert had developed a sense of what he thought was dramatically appropriate for the scene. "Performing on stage as entertainment" did not logically resonate with his notion of the "quiet and mysterious" tone of the meeting. Later in this entry, when commenting on my shady role, Albert confesses, "I don't want to trust him, which would make the story very much more exciting." Albert was functioning as both a playwright and director here, highlighting the unknown as an important element in process drama.

Other students were also distrusting of the mystery host. "Just like a classic story from Sir Arthur Conan Doyle," Tom wrote. As I read through their entries, I was enthralled by the stories that they were beginning to create for themselves. Meryl's doubts about the host bothered her, yet she was unsure of how to behave:

He seemed suspicious to me though because he didn't ask us for
our password he just stood there and I waited for us to say our
oath. . . . I was thinking to myself what Will had said he told us to
be very careful not to let the torres find out so I was wondering to
myself if he found out and killed him. But I couldn't act suspicious and I couldn't accuse him or approach him yet. I had
to find out more about him.

Some students were simply angry at Molineux's absence: "I had
known Will for many years," Amara wrote. "He is a responsible person, he should be here."

The writing was a useful forum for me to develop another perspective on how the students were responding to the drama. They
apparently were building commitment to their roles. Although not
all the students were distrusting of the stand-in for Molineux (Jessica and Selene, for instance, thought there was no convincing evidence to doubt him), it was clear that my manner had put a few on
their guard. The fact that some trusted me and some did not might
create tension later on. The situation for a dilemma was becoming
clearer: How would the patriots respond to a possible traitor in
their midst? In my log I contemplated that possibility:

They have willingly told me their oaths when they didn't know
who I was. I wonder whether I can turn their blind trust in me on
them in some way? I'm not sure how or when to do this. Much
of this will depend on how they interact during the role-play.

The group was obviously hooked into the drama. Although they were
interested in the current plot and in what was going to happen next,
I was keen to explore how the plot might be harnessed to challenge
their own decision making.

We are beginning to see how the perspectives being developed
from within the drama were facilitating a stronger commitment to
the work. The students were being challenged in more powerful
ways to consider the life of a patriot by creating that life, and living
it, than by just passively discussing it. This stance of being put in the
shoes of someone who was there, or who was paying witness to
events while they unfolded, is the great defining characteristic of
process drama. When students are placed within a dramatic world,
they can experience the struggles, the highs and lows, the conflicts
and dilemmas that might inhabit that world. When they begin to

experience these conditions, they can confront some quality of life that the drama is exploring, and from this experience learning can take place. Learning through drama then refers to the state of mind, or shifts in understanding, that the work ushers.

THE SECOND ENCOUNTER

I could not have predicted when the patriots' meeting, which I discussed earlier, resumed that the group would enthusiastically assume their roles and take actions for which they would have to accept responsibility. Throughout the process drama, I had endeavored to provide as many opportunities as I could for the students to assume ownership of the work. For the most part these tasks—whether in the form of devising tableaux of learning, formulating questions on a mysterious document, or creating a narrative of the patriots' journey through the streets of 1770 Boston—were completed over a relatively short time duration. The students' ownership reached new heights as the group indulged in spontaneous improvisation, what Bolton (1984) describes as dramatic play, for most of the following session. It was, as Albert later described, an "exhilarating" experience.

In my analysis of this session, I will isolate three sections of the transcribed encounter. The first focuses on the patriots' growing hostility toward the host; the second focuses on their decision as to what should be done; and the third focuses on the dilemma this decision posed.

The Patriots Grow in Hostility

Back in role as the mystery host, I invited the patriots to share some of their plans for dealing with the red menace, the lobsterbacks. We were seated in a haphazard arrangement. Albert had once again turned the lights out. Nadia was absent for this session, and Jessica did not participate, for she had been feeling ill throughout the morning. She was seated at the side resting her head on her arms.

TEDDY: We should put tar on them . . .
MADELENE: And then feather them.
PHIL: They might fight back if we put tar on them.
MERYL: Well, there's no reason why we can't fight them.
PHIL: They have guns you know.

MERYL: So do we.

PHIL: Are you saying we should be violent with them?

MERYL: Well, they're violent with us.

PHIL: I don't really see why . . . [I'm cut off in mid-sentence by an announcement from the principal's office]

PRINCIPAL (Over the public speaker): MAY I HAVE YOUR ATTENTION PLEASE. IT HAS BEGUN TO RAIN THEREFORE THERE WILL BE NO OUTSIDE YARD TODAY. THERE WILL BE NO YARD TODAY DUE TO THE RAIN. THANK YOU!

PHIL (Ignoring the announcement): I don't really see what purpose putting tar on their backs is going to achieve.

MERYL: Well, we have to do something given what they have been doing.

PHIL: Well, what have they done to us, these soldiers? They've done nothing to me personally. Have they done anything to you?

TEDDY: They kicked and whipped my brother.

PHIL: Was he putting tar on their backs?

TEDDY: They've got savage minds.

PHIL: So you think they're pretty violent.

ALBERT: They taxed my bullets.

PHIL: So? I mean a few taxes isn't going to hurt. Violence is . . .

MERYL: What have you got against violence?

PHIL: It's not that I'm against violence I'm just not sure . . .

MERYL: It sounds like you're for them.

PHIL: I'm not for them. I just don't want to get hurt.

MERYL (after a pause): So you want them to treat you like dirt!

PHIL: We could always go to the commissioner and tell him.

TEDDY: You could supply us with tar and we'll do it.

PHIL: Is this something you all want to be a party to? Put tar on the soldiers' backs?

TOM: Molasses!

PHIL: Well then [holding the eyes of many of the patriots]. When are we going to do this?

ALBERT: Friday next.

PHIL: Will thinks that these ships should somehow be prevented from entering Boston harbor. Will thinks we should try and stop them even landing here, these ships.

TEDDY: How about if we go to the wharf and just cut it into pieces and get them falling through.

PHIL: Yes, like a trap! [Pause. Examining Teddy] Have you done that before, have you? Are you the one I have read about sabotaging bridges and the like?

TOM: That was me!

PHIL: It was you, was it. Mmmm! I wonder what other things you've been up to. . . . [Looking at Madelene] Is this the first time you have come to this meeting?

MADELENE: Yes.

PHIL: What do you hope would come from this meeting?

MADELENE (Suspicious of the host): That nothing would happen.

PHIL: Something will happen.

MADELENE: Nothing will happen.

TOM: Not a true patriot!

PHIL: You're all patriots though aren't you?

MADELENE: Yes . . . [threateningly] Are you?

PHIL: How could you . . .

MERYL [Cutting off]: I don't trust you. [She stands]

PHIL: How could you question . . . of course I am. I let you in here, didn't I?

MERYL: Then how come we've never seen you before?

PHIL: I said my oath. I said the password.

MERYL: Well many know the password . . . and you could've just made that oath up. [A long pause]

PHIL: Would I do that?

MERYL [Slowly sitting down]: I don't know.

MADELENE [After a long pause]: Will said that all patriots should wear a white blouse.

TOM: Shirt!

PHIL [Pause. Pointing at my shirt, which has blue and white stripes]: I have some white here.

SUSAN: But not the white of the patriots!

TEDDY: It's supposed to be all white.

PHIL [I stand looking at their shirts, then at my own.]: You're all wearing white shirts . . . [Moving slowly to the imaginary door]

Although the transcribed section does not capture the nonverbal gestures, such as the restless movements and nervous twitches suggestive of the discomfort overcoming the patriots, it illuminates some of the key attitudes and stances taken. The section moves from a consideration of tactics to a questioning of the host's motivations. Teddy's responses are interesting in this respect. He focuses on tactics such as harassing the soldiers through abuse or sabotage, and even suggests that if I do not want to participate, perhaps I could supply them with the means to carry out the deed. Unlike Meryl, he does not immediately question my character. Instead, he tries to convince me that the soldiers are violent and have "savage minds." It takes him some time to recognize that the drama is no longer focusing on What are we going to do about the British soldiers? but on What are we going to do about this host's threatening presence?

Meryl, on the other hand, was suspicious from the beginning, when she strongly argued, much to the host's chagrin, that the patriots had convincing methods of dealing with the British. Her frustration, "we have to do something given what they have been doing," turns to doubt, "it sounds like you're for them," which later turns to incrimination, "I don't trust you." It was of interest to note the leading role Meryl was assuming. I wondered whether Nadia's and Jessica's nonparticipation were factors here, possibly enabling Meryl to have a focus she might not ordinarily have taken. The fact that she was also challenging the teacher-in-role suggested that she understood that in process drama this was possible: She would not be penalized for defying a teacher. Her courageous stance, "How come we've never seen you before?" seemed to encourage others to doubt. The students, in role as patriots, had to decide whether this issue was of sufficient importance to them. When Madelene finally revealed that the host was obviously duplicitous because he was not wearing a white shirt, her cohorts had to confront what this meant; what action, if any, would they now take?

"The basis of learning," Gardner (1965) once wrote, "is emotion" (34). While not wanting to undermine all of the recent interest in cognitive science, perhaps we might agree with Gardner that once the group's emotions were aroused, their decision taking assumed greater urgency. Gardner elaborates:

> There is no intellectual interest which does not spring from the need to satisfy feelings. . . . Not only is learning fostered by the need to satisfy feelings but feelings themselves are relieved and helped by learning. For work to be creative, feeling as well as intellect is involved. Any education must always take into account education of the emotions. (34)

The relationship between affect and cognition would become clearer as this session advanced.

The Decision

As the session continued and I walked to the door, Albert, holding his umbrella, aimed the weapon at me.

ALBERT [Preventing my escape]: No you don't.

TEDDY: Kill him. [Lots of animation now from the group]

PHIL [Looking at Albert's gun]: I wouldn't advise that you use that. [After a pause] I have to inform you all that this place will soon be surrounded. You will all be taken in as traitors to King George III. [Looks of disbelief] We have Molineux down at the courthouse.

MERYL: I knew it!

PHIL: He has confessed that he is a patriot. You have told me things here tonight that incriminate you all. You are all patriots. You are all traitors to King George III.

MERYL [Fed up]: That's enough! [To Albert] Shoot him!! [Frantic cries of "Kill him! Kill him!" They are all standing]

PHIL: Don't be ridiculous. The soldiers will be outside shortly. You can't escape. You are disloyal and treacherous to King George III. You'll be punished. Each and every one of you will be punished.

MERYL: Not if we can help it.

PHIL: You will be taken out into the streets like other traitors and be shot. [The group starts to crowd in on me]

PHIL: At last I have found out your secret oaths. This will put an end to all the patriot dealings in this town once and for all.

When the patriots started chanting "Kill him! Kill him!", reminding me of Jack and his tribe in Golding's *Lord of the Flies*, I dropped the role.

PHIL: Is he dead? Did you shoot him?

GROUP [Excitedly]: Yes!

PHIL [Narrating]: So, before the traitor could leave the house he was shot to death. The bloodied body of the traitor was left at the door. The patriots had to decide . . .

ALBERT [cutting me off]: Had to plan!

PHIL [Incorporating Albert's idea]: Had to plan what they were going to do. Make your plan.

While I was satisfying the patriots' desire for "blood," as an educator I was searching for a way, as Heathcote (1975) says, to help them "confront their own actions and decisions" (87). The patriots had decided to murder the host. What consequences might this stance have?

My transition from my being in role to out of role seemed a smooth one and was readily accepted by the group. Some commentators (Burgess and Gaudry 1985; Morgan and Saxton 1987) have argued that a scenario such as the above, which has been described as "Kill the King," can quickly end a drama because the process drama cannot develop from this point. In our case, it appeared to be the vehicle through which the students encountered a real dilemma.

The Dilemma and Its Implications

While seated at the rear of the room I watched and listened as the patriots made a plan. Later, it was difficult for me to transcribe this section of the tape because of the lively and spirited talk. In a sense, I welcomed this difficulty because it indicated energetic commitment to the task.

MERYL [Sits in the chair the traitor had been in. Assuming command]: Alright . . . How many of you have weapons? [She counts those who raise their hands]. One . . . two . . . three . . . do you [looking at Teddy] have a weapon or not?

TEDDY: No. . . . Time's running out.

MERYL: They don't know that he's dead yet so they can't plan.

ALBERT: We can pretend that we're Tories.

TEDDY: We'll hide up there [pointing to the ceiling] in the light.

ALBERT: What light? A candle you mean.

TOM: It's not going to work.

MERYL: What suggestions do you have, Tom?

TOM: How do you know that there are soldiers outside?

ALBERT: Pretend that we're Tories and that we killed him.

MERYL: But how do they know that we're a Tory?

ALBERT [Points to his gun]: Taxed bullets!

MERYL: Make a suggestion, Tom.

TOM: We should run out and kidnap . . .

TEDDY: No, kill them.

MERYL: But not all of us have weapons.

SUSAN: There might be a secret passageway.

MERYL: If there was a secret doorway . . . we could hide in there until they leave

TOM [After a long pause]: I know what we should do . . . go to the attic . . . find the window . . . and climb out to the Liberty Tree, slowly make our way down and run for our lives.

MERYL: One of us should get out and call the other patriots. [pause] Any volunteers?

ALBERT [Directed at Meryl]: We nominate you.

Fueling their decision making with further tension, I layered in a narrative link: "And in the distance you saw British soldiers walking down the road heading toward the house. Those soldiers were going to be coming through that door any minute."

TOM: I told you what we should do and that is go down the Liberty Tree.

TEDDY: Why don't we all just run out.

MERYL [After a pause]: One of us could dress like him [pointing to the imaginary dead man] . . . one of the boys and pretend that we're him.

TOM: But that's only one of us.

MERYL [Frustrated]: Well, who's got a better idea?

TOM: I told you my idea. Climb out to the Liberty Tree.

MERYL: Well, what's the vote.

It was a demanding task for them to make a decision. They canvassed a number of possibilities: hiding in the ceiling, finding a secret doorway, climbing down the Liberty Tree, dressing up as a Tory, and shooting the soldiers. It was frustrating for them to select one. Each possibility had merits, so it was therefore a complex choice. Occasionally they would look my way for assistance, probably hoping that the teacher would provide the correct answer; but the looks over time became less frequent. Perhaps they realized that there was no correct answer. As Verhovek (1991) has argued, often in social studies it can be questionable whether the teacher's solution is more valid than the children's, since the teacher's view may have no better factual or analytic basis than the children being taught.

The group now encountered a number of options, each equally attractive. "Intellectual development," Bruner (1966) suggests, "is marked by an increasing capacity to deal with several alternatives simultaneously" (6). When Meryl hastily convened a vote as though this would automatically solve the problem, I hoped the group would become aware of the possible implications of their decision. The majority had voted on Tom's plan.

> MERYL: All right, so we'll climb out the Liberty Tree.
>
> PHIL [After a long pause. Slowly. Deliberately.]: So, you leave the traitor's body there?
>
> TOM: Yea. [Others agree]
>
> PHIL [Reinforcing my question]: You leave that bloodied Tory's body at the doorstep of this house?
>
> MERYL: Yea, and Teddy can put his sign ["No Lobsterbacks"] on it.
>
> PHIL: Does everyone agree to that? [Chorus of "yes"]
>
> MERYL: And with the sign on it.
>
> TOM [Pleased]: An intimidation!
>
> PHIL [Thoughtfully]: You then incriminate this house, William Molineux's house, as being a meeting place for the patriots? [Pause. Long pause. They had not considered this] Is that what you want to do? [Deathly silence]

There have been rare moments in my teaching life where I have stumbled upon either a question or a statement that noticeably rocks students' thinking. I could not have predicted that in this session such a moment as this would occur. The dilemma the students were now in was powerful. If they escaped from the house and left the body behind, they might put Molineux, a friend and respected fellow patriot, in greater danger than he already was. Immediate self-interest versus possible disloyalty appeared to be an issue here. Would they become traitors to Molineux if they escaped and left the body? What are the personal costs of loyalty?

In the ensuing silence, the group appeared to be constructing their own meaning of the events they had just witnessed and particularly their own role in those events. Awareness, Donalson (1978) argues, typically develops when something gives us pause:

> And when consequently, instead of just acting, we stop to consider the possibilities of acting which are before us. The claim is that we heighten our awareness of what is actual by considering what is possible. We are conscious of what we do to the extent that we are conscious of what we do not do—of what we might have done. The notion of choice is thus central. (97)

Learning through process drama gives rise to moments when leaders and students must make choices, and accept responsibility for those choices.

When Meryl suggested that the traitor might not be dead after all, it was agreed that Teddy should go and check the pulse. After slowly walking up to the imaginary body, lifting the arm, and searching for a pulse, Teddy would confirm the death. After the session, I regretted not encouraging all the patriots to have felt the pulse. The implications of the death needed to be highlighted and all the frightening consequences of their involvement and decision making understood. Otherwise, I reasoned, the drama might simply become a bloodthirsty adventure rather than a push toward higher-order thinking.

Although the patriots now understood that they could not simply leave the body behind, they were still undecided about what to do. Their journal writing that evening reflected their uncertainty. Meryl wrote:

> We had no choice we had to kill him or else we would have been captured and torchered by the torres. . . . We had to think positive and make a plan fast. . . . Some suggested that we take them on but god knows how many of them their are were only twelve. . . . In my opinion the best plan was to take the soldier with us and get rid of all the evidence that might give them a clue then we could climb out the window to the Liberty Tree and make a run for it and then tell the torres that we have him and stall for time to think of a plan to rescue Will Moldono.

Their contemplative thoughts suggested they were emotionally tied into the process drama. "If I had the choice to change and start the meeting again," Amara wrote, "I wouldn't reveal the plot to that tori and wouldn't kill him, just capture him . . . and trade him for William." This thinking through the implications of the patriots' actions reached poetic levels, as Tom's entry suggests:

> It was dark, very, very dark. I heard a voice. This shy person asked us (the patriots) all of our secrets. Just to find out that he wasn't William Molineaux he was the mystery person that I have been writing about in my past few journals. This host was nothing but a hoax. He tricked us and was about to get away. Until . . . bang, Bang, BANG . . . as the gun of the patriotic silversmith shot out

"bullets of death." Thus, came the panic. We had nowhere to run, but to hide. What beholds us in the future I nor my fellow patriots know. Maybe our names could be in the town newspapers for being so heroic, or on a tombstone. "Nuff" said till next time . . .

It was illuminating to note the different ways in which each student responded to the traitor's murder. Some regretted the patriots' actions; others, like Albert, applauded them. They were constructing their own personal meanings of the encounter based on their immediate reading of it. Tom, for instance, passionately felt that Meryl had broken her patriot's oath during the Molineux meeting. He cited her candor with the host, such as her telling of patriots' tactics for dispensing with the British. He maintained that she had violated the patriots' vow of silence that was expressed in her oath.

"Isn't Meryl supposed to rot?" he asked. Meryl quickly dismissed this with a sharp, "Shut up! Tom." However, the issue of obligation to principles was one Tom would constantly raise. "She revealed the plot!" Tom gleefully told Nadia on her return to class the next week. "The whole enchilada," he went on. Despite Jessica's defense, "She didn't know that he was a soldier though," Tom was still dissatisfied. "She's not doing it on purpose," Nadia concluded, supporting her friend. "She thought it was somebody else." I listened with interest as they would challenge, dismiss, and support one another's ideas. Tom wouldn't budge. His final words on the subject, "So much for a loyal patriot!" were curtly expressed in his journal.

Teachers, it has been argued, have to honor and respect the meaning students apply to events:

> In the interest of making connections between their understanding and ours, we must adopt an insider's view: seek to understand their sense as well as help them understand ours. (Duckworth 1987, 112)

Although I thought Tom was being partly provocative in his condemnation of Meryl, an antagonistic role he would often play, the question of responsibilities and commitments had prompted a thoughtful discussion. When I reminded Tom that every patriot revealed his or her oath willingly to the host, despite the suspicions of some, we considered the issue of trust and acceptance. When I asked them why nobody attempted to prevent the killing of the traitor, we considered the issue of mob mentality. This problem led into a revealing discussion of how people can sometimes get caught up in events over which they have no control. When I asked why nobody thought through the consequences of his or her murderous actions, Meryl said, "We didn't have time." Albert concurred, "We were too happy." Emotions as a major factor in decision making were resonating here.

As we examined some of the general issues that their actions raised, the question of historical interpretation became central. Ironically, Nadia's absence helped accentuate the different perspectives of the meeting. As the group attempted to explain on her return what happened in the session, it was apparent that individual values affected these explanations. Whether or not an oath was violated was one example of this lack of objectivity. Whether the patriots' actions were justifiable was another. Which of the plans for dispensing with the body was the more helpful was yet another. Albert suggested that the events are told as they are "saw." When I asked him to elaborate on this idea, he suggested, for example, that if a person attending that meeting at Molineux's was sympathetic to the British or in fact "was a Tory it might describe us as bad hooligans or something like and that we were plotting malice or trying to cause trouble for the British . . . make life hard for them."

The argument was compellingly being made that even though we all attended the same meeting there would be a range of interpretations depending on our political, cultural, and social perspectives. Nadia's journal contemplations about the meeting—"Two of my closest friends were involved. I wonder if they're scared?"—highlighted how individual loyalties might affect perspectives. This notion, that we give meaning to events rather than receive meaning from them, seems an important pedagogical principle in that it helps participants understand the role they play in constructing knowledge. It is this idea of *giving meaning to* that is at the heart of learning through process drama.

When Albert read aloud more of Phelan's book, from which we had taken the Molineux meeting scenario, Nadia was surprised about Samuel Adams's belief in "dignified non-co-operation." It suggested to her that Adams might not have supported the tactics used in our imagined meeting. Nevertheless, Albert emphasized that this was not a view that all patriots shared: "Molineux wants to use force and weapons to get rid of the soldiers." We compared our imagined enacted version of a historical encounter with the recorded one. "Our meeting was more exciting," Nadia said, even though she was not present for it. "There was more things happening: People had come a long way through the dark and everything. They described problems they had." Teddy agreed. "It was more lively," he said. "You can see what's going on and then make it up as you go along." Simply reading about the event would not help Teddy "see what's going on."

The students' reactions indicated that the experience of participating in the process drama was a powerful one for them. As I reflected on their responses to our Molineux meeting, and about the nature of history and the value of drama, I was reminded of Heathcote (1980a):

> I have struggled to perfect techniques which allow my classes
> opportunities to stumble upon authenticity in their work and to
> be able both to experience and reflect upon their experience
> at the same time: simultaneously to understand their journey while
> being both the cause and the medium of the work. (11)

I was troubled, however, that we had not fully explored the soldiers' plight. We had built up an identification with the patriots' cause. This bond had developed when the motivations of William LeBaron were considered earlier. Although the hardships and crises generally faced by the patriots were important, it was only one aspect of the Boston Massacre story. To completely focus on the patriots' view, I thought, would confirm the stereotypically oppressive image of the soldiers created by the picture Adams had circulated of the Boston Massacre.

I was especially concerned with some of the impressions that the students had formed of the soldiers. "The British are very annoying," wrote Albert, in role as a patriot sympathizer. "They walk all over town and makes our eyes sore, and speak and walk as if they were any better of us." Not only were the soldiers' presumed arrogance and egocentricities being highlighted for criticism, but also their potential for committing violent acts was emphasized as well. "Soldiers threatened the boys," Susan declared, "saying that they'll bash their skulls." The British regiments behaved, according to Tom, in "cruel and unworthy" ways. Joyce agreed, arguing that the redcoats "always started the fights between the colonists and themselves."

Parker (1991) has suggested that social studies educators must avoid promoting "narrow or ethnocentric" viewpoints in the classroom. Although he notes that the discipline of social studies is a controversial one in that "reasonable people will disagree on a great many issues," he believes that teachers must press students into "higher-order work" (84). Such is characterized, Parker further asserts, by a "compendium" of intellectual tasks:

> comparing and contrasting examples, seeking out exceptions to rules, posing questions and hypotheses, analyzing the values that fuel controversies, exploring and clarifying perspectives that are different from one's own, adding relief to the terrain with rich historical literature, interrogating one's conclusions. (96)

Earlier I maintained that one of the reasons for my being drawn to the Boston Massacre was that it presented at least two distinct and contrasting viewpoints: those represented by the soldiers compared with those of the patriots. The period was potentially rich for exploring opposing perspectives. Students, I hoped, would struggle with these contrasts and potential contradictions and ambiguities, perhaps using them as a springboard when forming their own.

Yet the perspectives that the class had developed were predominantly supportive of the patriots' cause. This value was a structural problem: The work had been heavily weighted in favor of the patriots. In a sense, there was a danger that we might have romanticized the life of the Boston Whigs as they faced cloak-and-dagger meetings and pursued adventurous exploits. The work, some might argue, had a "comic strip" quality, not reaching wider political and social issues that perhaps resonated at that time.

Historians, for instance, have stressed that the soldiers stationed in Boston were victims of constant physical and psychological terror (Kidder 1870; Sobel et al. 1982). The often fanatical tactics of the radical group known as the Sons of Liberty, including such vandalism as the desecration of public property, were pitched at undermining the soldiers' authority (Phelan 1976). Zobel (1970) has argued that one of the intriguing aspects of the Boston Massacre is that Captain Preston and the eight soldiers accused of murdering the five colonists were considered by the jury to be innocent. Although two soldiers were found guilty of manslaughter, it was extraordinary, Zobel asserts, that given the hostile "blood for blood" atmosphere in Boston, all the prisoners were eventually released (299).

The defendants, under the guidance of a distinguished counselor, John Adams, had successfully proved that they were acting in self-defense: They had been unduly provoked and subjected to inhumane and ruthless treatment at the hands of some colonists. Although Zobel stresses that this verdict clearly reveals Boston to be a "Cradle of Liberty" in pre-Revolutionary society, I thought that the process drama had not yet fully addressed the soldiers' story, a story pivoting, it seemed, on victimization and harassment. It had not successfully reached Parker's criteria for "higher-order work."

TEACHER AS ARTIST

Learning through process drama then demands that leaders are conscious of the kinds of meanings students are giving to events. To end our process drama with the death of the traitor, while challenging the students to take responsibility for their actions, was distorting the relationship between the patriots and the governing forces. Recorded history suggests that the soldiers were not always the villains of the period. How could I help the students understand this position through our work? How could I manipulate the curriculum to find balance?

These questions, dealing as they do with both the content and the form of the piece, are reminiscent of those concerns artists grapple with as they attempt to render meaning. Process drama teachers are constantly searching for balance and harmony and other aesthetic qualities so that what is created is pleasing and satisfying for all of the participants.

Process drama workers share with artists a desire to achieve clarity and purpose through the manipulation of form. Such desire may result in old ideas being rethought and new ideas being introduced. Experimenting with different strategies and techniques characterizes the process drama teacher's craft; some of these experiments might be illuminating, others might not be helpful at all. Not only is what is said through the work critical (the content of process drama), but also the manner in which the content is rendered (the form of process drama). This concern with form and content clearly locates process drama within an artistic domain.

For the rest of the chapter I will describe how my interest in balance and harmony led to the introduction of new material, and how this material aimed to provide yet another perspective on the work.

Making Connections

When I asked the class, "How do you think the soldiers might have felt about being in Boston?" Nadia responded, "They probably didn't want to be there" because "nobody likes looking for trouble." Joyce agreed. She had read that the soldiers were only there in the first place "to protect the officials." The colonists, Albert further asserted, had been "revolting the government" in that "they were burning the stamps and not following the laws." The germ of an idea—that the soldiers might just have been doing their job—was starting to take root.

When Jessica proposed a possible parallel between today's police force and the eighteenth-century Boston guard, I reflected upon the means through which we could explore the soldiers' claims that they were acting in self-defense. In doing so, I hoped I would be responding to Parker's call for curricula that challenges narrow historical interpretations.

"Drama for discovery," Heathcote (1975) once argued, "is not about ends; it is about journeys and not knowing how the journeys may end" (86). One effective method for illuminating that journey can be to devise a similar or analogous situation to the one being examined. This strategy might be useful for exploring how people react when they experience harassment. A contemporary scene of an individual being persecuted might assist the students in their contemplations of the Boston soldiers' predicament. In this respect analogies, Heathcote (1984) maintains, have the advantage "of making something fresh and worthy of consideration when it has become too cliché-ridden, too familiar, too full of prejudice because of memory and past weariness. It provides a new face for old material" (207).

After devoting two sessions to preparing a modern-day improvisation that revealed an individual being persecuted, the group watched with interest as Selene, Joyce, Amara, and Brenda shared their scene. This was the first time in the process drama that these four girls had worked together as a unit. While observing their rehearsal process, I had noticed the spirited manner in which they responded to the task. "They obviously are very relaxed working with each other," I wrote in my log. "I've noticed that when Tom or Nadia work with them, they appear reticent to contribute, perhaps feeling intimidated by the way both can seemingly dictate proceedings."

Selene had written in her journal that students should work in familiar groups, in which "they could feel less shy and more talkable." Such an arrangement, she argued, would help them "work together and comfortably." As these girls eagerly assumed their opening positions, I felt that their "flow of lively talk" in rehearsal was generated by their mutual friendship. What was striking, however, in their improvisation was the brutality that they were portraying, a marked contrast to their reserved demeanors that I perceived in the classroom.

Selene, assuming the role of an ostracized school student, was sitting alone, while the other three "bullies" surrounded her. "Hi, little girl!" Amara sniggered, leaning over the front of Selene's desk. Joyce and Brenda sat beside the terrorized victim. "Do you have the money?" persisted Amara. After Selene nervously whispered, "No," Amara uncharacteristically thumped the desk with both fists. "If you don't give me the money, you won't see your parents ever again," she bellowed. With that brash show of force, Selene attempted to leave, but the bodyguards pushed her back in the seat. She reluctantly surrendered her money.

"Oh my god!" Nadia exclaimed at the scene's conclusion, hardly believing, it seemed, that these four girls would reenact a moment with such venom. "She tried to get away," Meryl interjected, referring to Selene, "but the others beat her up." The students decided to examine this scene further to determine what alternatives the victim might have had in overcoming her harassment. Each group was invited to reenact the four girls' improvisation. This procedure, I suggested, would help us examine how different people might deal with a similar kind of oppression.

"Got any money?" threatened Jessica, assuming Amara's role. "No," retorted Teddy, playing the victim. "Are you sure?" she asked, while Susan and Madelene searched him forcefully for valuables. Teddy surrendered to the assault. "They grabbed the money!" Amara said in disbelief after the scene had finished. "Teddy," she continued, drawing a distinction from Selene, "didn't give" it over. The bullies, Nadia proposed, describing the roles of Madelene and Susan, "were a lot more rougher" than in the original scene.

"Do you think," I asked, "that Teddy could have done anything to change his state of victimization?" Albert had an idea, "He might have just freely given them the money." By willingly offering his wallet, Albert thought, Teddy might be able to get the attackers to withdraw quietly. I suggested that the group replay the scene, but this time Teddy would incorporate Albert's suggestion. The bullies, however, only seemed more determined. After snatching his cash, they fiendishly removed Teddy's watch, and then, adding insult to injury, stole his glasses. "It made it worse," Nadia observed, commenting on Albert's suggestion.

"We took advantage," Jessica concluded, implying that there were no simple solutions to overcoming victimization. Meryl, like Nadia, believed this scene was "more rougher." Tom disagreed. "There wasn't," he argued, "as much physical contact" as when Selene had been violently forced back into her desk. "Do you think," I asked, "physical abuse is more harmful than mental and psychological abuse?" The group seemed divided on this question. "I think mental," suggested Joyce, "because you could hurt people's feelings." Teddy shook his head, seemingly disagreeing, although he did not respond verbally. "Is it possible," I pressed, "to overcome victimization?" Meryl thought it was if "you go and tell other people." Nadia agreed, maintaining that one way might be to "try and get big people on your side."

"Experience," Bolton (1979) argues, "is neither productive nor unproductive; it is how you reflect on it that makes it significant or not" (126). As we canvassed a range of possible strategies for how these seventh graders might deal with victimization, and then attempted to work these out through dramatic action, it seemed evident that there were no saccharin or magical solutions. The same dilemma might be worked through in a variety of ways, if at all. This awareness, I hoped, might be illuminating when we considered the soldiers' actions during the Boston Massacre. Although the soldiers may have had alternatives to shooting the colonists, would these be viable ones?

Boal (1985) argues that one of the strengths of dramatic activity is that it can help participants explore in action the "possible paths" through which crises can be resolved. Meryl seemed to agree with Boal when she later argued that in drama "there is no wrong answer; it is just what you think." Although the analogous incident had raised questions of how people respond when harassed, we needed to explore more concretely the factors influencing the soldiers' decisions to shoot. My concern, though, was How can we address this issue while remaining alert to the intense passions and "blood for blood" feelings that pervaded eighteenth-century Boston?

Making Plans

Readers will note how throughout this work I am consciously grappling with what makes for good lesson planning and execution. There is a constant process of reevaluating my aims and procedures and eagerly searching for the appropriate strategies that will help promote the learning. In a sense, this search and re-search is not unlike the approach artists pursue as they experiment with ideas and seek clarity.

Occasionally, these searches can be unproductive or lead to errors in execution. However, leaders of process drama should not be worried when things don't seem to work as had been hoped. As I was to discover with these seventh graders, the best-laid plans can often go astray when faced with the demands of the immediacy of a dramatic encounter. For instance, as I was trying to find a context in which the students could begin to empathize with the soldiers' position in Boston, my planning could be described as shabby and ill-informed.

The students in this flawed session had been discussing the atmosphere in Boston on the evening of March 5, 1770, when the five colonists were killed. The discussion had focused on the anger, tension, and revenge that might have existed in the township. Albert thought "lynching" aptly described how some patriots would like to deal with the soldiers. I had given each student an office file with the title *Junior Counselor* on the cover. Inside was an eyewitness's account of the events of March 5. My structural thinking was that the students might assume the roles of attorneys representing the soldiers at the trial. Inexperienced lawyers, I presumed, are rarely experts, and therefore the students would not need to have at their fingertips explicit details of the case. At the same time, the role suggested an inquiry stance, which might help the students speculate and form opinions on questions about the soldiers' guilt.

I began with the words, "Rather than me tell you who we might be in this drama let's try and find our roles during the work." I noticed at the time that the group looked baffled, which should have signaled to me that a renegotiation was needed, but I foolishly ignored the signals. "Just pick up my signals," I vaguely continued, "and play it as you think you might."

"You can't get away with shabby planning," Heathcote (1984) said of classroom teaching. My obscure instruction, "play it as you think you might," was, in hindsight, too general. When I assumed the role of a reluctant Junior Counselor, I was not clearly signaling to the group the context. "Well," I confidently commenced the drama, "I don't know what you think about all of this, but I'm not very happy at being here." I slouched back in the chair, hoping that this role would be viewed less authoritatively than the supervisor's or the mystery host's. "These guys," I continued, waving my file, "have willfully gone into the streets and shot down those colonists, and yet we're expected to assist John Adams and prepare a defense." I thought the scenario was now becoming clearer and would enable them to participate.

"I don't know whether you saw this picture in the *Boston Gazette*," I declared, holding up the engraving of the Boston Massacre. "These soldiers have cold-bloodedly shot those colonists down. Now we are expected to defend them. Impossible!" The picture was now being passed around from counselor to counselor. Still, no one was contributing verbally. "I mean," I sighed, "I don't know what you see in that picture but all I see is," I provocatively announced, "a willful and calculated act of murder." The students seemed confused. "Sam Adams has circulated so many of these pictures in this town. How are we supposed to get a fair trial in this city? It's pointless." Silence. Perhaps they agreed with me. Pointless!

In my log that evening, I likened my role-play to a "comic who doesn't get any laughs." I asked, "Do you continue in the hope that eventually someone may enter, or stop and say, 'see ya next time,' while mincing off stage?" In this instance, I decided to cease the role-play because I couldn't "read" their silence: Was it because of confusion or were there other factors? "Mr. Taylor, I didn't know who we were," criticized Nadia. "Were we representing the soldiers or the colonists?" Her admission troubled me. Albert, on the other hand, later wrote that he thought the class was verbally passive in the drama because "we didn't know how to approach it without calling attention to ourselves. I presume we didn't want to stand out, didn't really know what to do, not used to discussing issues."

"I think," Madelene offered, disagreeing with Nadia, "that we were there as people who were going to help John Adams prepare a case to defend the soldiers." She thought, however, that I was role-playing John Adams. "No," Nadia interrupted, rethinking the drama now. She decided that I was "one of the people who was helping" Adams. Our spirited analysis of what was happening in the role-play seemed to help clarify the drama. "You were one of us," she continued. "The one out of everybody who always talked and asked questions."

Now that the contexts of the drama were clearer, I decided that it might be fruitful to return to the role-play. This time, however, the counselors would process some of the issues surrounding the case. They each read their file and imagined that they had interviewed the witness who gave the deposition. Although the counselors had different accounts of the massacre, the depositions all were sympathetic to the soldiers.

When we returned to the drama, the counselors appeared to have a firm agenda, and they were not as willing to accept the negativity that I initially continued to express:

PHIL: I'm not too happy about being here at all.

ALBERT: Well, we're supposed to help the soldiers.

PHIL: They've been accused of shooting down the soldiers in cold blood.

ALBERT: It was only rumors.

PHIL: There were soldiers shot. There are no rumors there.

ALBERT: Then it would be self-defense.

PHIL: How are you going to prove self-defense when everybody hates the British soldiers?

ALBERT: We get people to testify . . . I just want to defend them . . . [Holds up his file] Dr. John Jeffries!

PHIL: He attended one of the guys that was shot, didn't he?

ALBERT: Yes, and even the person shot said that it was in self-defense. . . . The people were mobbing the soldiers, throwing oyster shells and ice, and the soldiers went back in. . . . John Adams is doing the right thing.

PHIL: Not in my book.

TOM [Doubtful of my stance]: What is the right thing? What is the right thing?

PHIL: The right thing is that . . . Sam Adams, John Adams's cousin, had this picture circulated. [I hold the Boston Massacre picture up] These soldiers should be taken out and given the same treatment.

TOM: But you gotta look on the other side. These people were crowding them. They could have been hurt very badly like . . . the boy I spoke with justified that a soldier was hit by a patriot.

PHIL [pointing to the picture]: It doesn't look like anybody's crowding around the soldiers there.

NADIA [Agreeing with me]: I know. There's only eight of them and they're killing them all. . . . They're all going to be talking about us.

MERYL [Challenging Nadia]: So why did you come here in the first place?

NADIA: Hey, listen babe!

As the drama unfolded, the counselors shared some of the information they had collected. Counselor Joyce had spoken with James Brewer. "He said," she told her peers, "the soldiers were teased. They had things thrown at them." Brewer's testimony could be corroborated. A captain by the name of Goldfinch, Meryl claimed, supporting Joyce, had been provoked by some colonists who had "spat at him."

The evidence was mounting for a claim of self-defense. Nadia was changing her mind about the case. "The best thing we have to go on," she now argued, "is to keep bringing up the subject the colonists gave the soldiers a hard time." Other counselors seemed to agree. Although I conceded feeling "nervous" about taking the case on, Tom's argument that lawyers must "protect" their clients, particularly when they are unjustly accused, was convincing. This principle may mean taking a stand that the general population did not sanction. "I guess when you're a lawyer," Nadia surmised, "you just have to put up with these things."

The "shabby" beginning to the whole-group drama had transformed, after we isolated some of its weaknesses, into an effective medium for the students to sift through, synthesize, and classify the key issues in building a defense. The drama created a context, I believed, wherein this defense building would not be a simple task for the counselors. "They probably think I am a traitor," Teddy wrote, in role as the defendants' attorney, describing the Boston populace. "But," he further declared, "I don't care about critizism, all I care is justice for innocent people."

Some counselors already thought that they were being harshly singled out for taking on the case. "When I walk down the street," Amara wrote in her log, "no one speaks or looks at me because now I assist John Adams." The "whispering" and "strange lookings" of the townsfolk would greet Madelene, too, on her travels through Boston. "My family and I will be dipped into the Mill Pond for sure," contemplated Albert, if he were to "announce in public" that he was working with John Adams. What a different perspective they were now forming, I thought, from when they so eagerly embraced LeBaron's depictions of the soldiers' barbarism in earlier work.

A report of the National Council for the Social Studies Task Force (1989) recommends a "holistic-interactive" approach to curricula planning (376). Content, the Task Force argued, should be presented in ways that provide "a comprehensive view of a complex whole." As the seventh graders contemplated the challenges of lawyers preparing a defense, they seemed to acknowledge how complex such a duty was, especially in light of the hostile passions circulating at the time. When Teddy later conceded that the Boston Massacre contained "right on both sides: the colonists shouldn't be throwing snowballs at the soldiers and the soldiers shouldn't fire at them," he was apparently grappling with some of the contradictory forces that the Task Force promotes. At twelve years of age, Teddy seemed to be contemplating his own "understanding" of the massacre. In a journal entry created in role as an eyewitness to the massacre, Teddy wrote:

> I was in a hous with 4 of my friends, when we heard the church bells ringing. We all ran out trying to put the fire out but when we got out, there was no fire. Then we saw a crowd of people down the street, so I decided to go there + see what was the matter. When I got there I saw Lobsterbacks + wiggs were arguing. Then a barber's boy came to a sentinel + told him "You son of a bitch knocked me down." When the crowd heard this they started yelling, "Kill him, kill him."

Just as qualitative researchers perceive reality in multiple and shifting ways (Ely et al. 1991; Ely et al. 1997), comprehensive historical inquirers also require standpoints that accept diverse and multidimensional conceptions of reality. I assumed that the process drama would also have to accommodate an array of standpoints. The students' reality of where the onus of guilt lay in the Boston Massacre, for example, was marked by varying conclusions. Joyce argued that simply because the soldiers were harassed did not justify their "right to fire," whereas Madelene maintained that they had to shoot to "save" themselves. Although the drama could not resolve these differences, it was able to highlight and challenge them. One effective strategy was to analyze critically, through role-play, the testimony of those who witnessed the King Street shootings in Boston.

Revealing Complexities: Hot Seating

Putting students in the "hot seat," wherein "character's motivations and personality" are questioned, is a common strategy in process drama (Neelands 1990, 28). In our case, the students assumed the role of eyewitnesses, preparing for their cross-examination in court. This strategy was appealing to me, for it might reveal the complexity of historical reconstruction. When Teddy wrote, as an eyewitness, his version of the events of March 5, 1770, I wondered what conclusions could be drawn from the events he recounts. What historical reality was he sharing? How do we know that we can trust his version? Where might we question the evidence he presents?

The witnesses, the students in role, were informed that the prosecution would attempt to "find the weaknesses" in their testimony when they appeared in court. John Adams's secretary, the teacher-in-role, explained that they would need "to get a feel" for what it would be like when they were "standing up in that courtroom" by themselves. Nadia agreed to be the first witness to role-play her testimony being challenged. After assuming the hot seat, she calmly recalled how she saw some boys "tearing down the butcher's stall" until they fixed their eyes on a sentinel. These boys, she exclaimed, then commenced "calling the sentinel names until he got fed up and hit them."

The witnesses and Adams's secretary, role-playing crown prosecutors, listened intently as Nadia spoke, and searched diligently for contradictions in her story:

TOM: How many boys were there?
NADIA: I don't know . . . I can't remember.
PHIL: You can't remember how many boys there were?
NADIA: No!
PHIL [Rapidly]: Were there Ten? Twenty? Fifty?
NADIA: Less than that.
PHIL: Less than what? Ten?
NADIA: Less than ten, yea.
PHIL: Less than ten boys?

NADIA: Maybe four or five.

TOM: Alright. Let me get this straight. A soldier, having a gun, swipes four or five people with the back of it at the same time. You couldn't have the strength.

NADIA: What?

TOM [Questioning her account]: A soldier couldn't hit five people with a gun at the same time. I don't know how anybody could have the strength.

NADIA: I didn't say he hit them all at the same time.

TOM [Modeling a complex physical act]: So! One at a time like this, and then this, and this . . . nobody could do that.

PHIL: How many did he hit?

NADIA: How many?

PHIL: Yes.

NADIA: He hit the ones that were . . . there were only . . . he probably hit like two of them. I don't think he hit all of them.

PHIL: Do you call hitting people with a bayonet fair tactics?

NADIA: No, but I don't call making fun of the sentinel fair either.

TOM: So, he did hit them with a bayonet!

NADIA: Yea a gun.

PHIL: With the knife at the end of his gun?

NADIA: No, he hit them with the back. The part you hold on with.

PHIL: Did you try to stop it?

NADIA: No.

PHIL: Why not?

NADIA: Because I might have been hit.

PHIL: So you stayed there and you watched.

NADIA: No, I was passing by . . . and didn't stop and watch it, or anything, I was passing by.

PHIL: You passed by, you didn't stay and see what was going to happen?

NADIA: No.

PHIL: Is this a normal occurrence in Boston, a riot, that you would pass by and not watch?

NADIA: [Pause. Frustrated] I don't know.

Drama, Heathcote (1975) maintains, is often powered by the "state of being trapped, a state from which one can escape only by working through the situation" (79). Other witnesses, like Nadia, were being challenged on their memory of specific details. Susan, admitting that she believed the soldiers were provoked, had to remember carefully whether Captain Preston gave the order to shoot. "Everyone was yelling 'Fire,'" she asserted, "they just fired." She described a scene of bedlam: "After they fired, I just ran."

The pressure of intense questioning seemed to create confusion in the mind of one witness:

BRENDA: I was a few yards away from the scene . . . Captain Preston was telling the soldiers to go home and stop shooting, and stuff like that.

PHIL: So, the soldiers were actually shooting at the patriots?

NADIA: And you were a few yards away?

TOM: And you could hear him say that?

BRENDA: Yea, I was only three or four yards away.

PHIL: Did the soldiers go home?

BRENDA: No, I think they didn't listen.

PHIL: Are you going to tell the court that the soldiers are ruthless killers?

BRENDA [Unsure]: I guess, because they didn't listen to Captain Preston.

NADIA: What were the colonists doing to the soldiers?

BRENDA: I don't think they were doing anything.

TOM: So, how do you know that the soldiers shot at the colonists if you didn't see them?

BRENDA: I was only a few yards away so I didn't see the whole thing.

NADIA [confused by her answer]: Yea, but you saw the shooting. Who were they shooting at?

BRENDA: The soldiers were shooting at the patriots.

ALBERT: You saw that? [Brenda nods]

PHIL: Did Captain Preston give the order to fire?

BRENDA: No, he was telling them to stop shooting and . . .

ALBERT: What were his exact words?

BRENDA: Ummm [pause] . . . "Stop Shooting."

NADIA: If you heard Captain Preston tell the soldiers to stop shooting, how come you didn't hear anything the colonists were saying?

BRENDA: Ummm . . . I just saw them shooting. I don't really know what was going on.

JESSICA: Did you get there after the colonists might have done something, or you got there right at the point in which the soldiers were shooting? (Brenda doesn't answer)

PHIL [Pause]: Are you sure you're telling the whole truth?

JESSICA: I think she's a liar.
NADIA: You are under oath you know.
BRENDA: That's all I remember.

Whose version of history can we trust? How does one determine provocation? Why are the "exact words" important? What part does the retelling of events play in history's reconstruction? The students were seemingly struggling with these questions as they listened to the various testimonies. "Are you a patriot or a loyalist?" Jessica would later ask Tom, hinting that political sympathies may influence a perception. How can one separate the argument from the person? Truth from deception? Reality from fantasy?

Using the hot seat enabled us to explore some of these issues, particularly when a witness, like Brenda, was perceived as equivocating. Her reluctance to tell the "whole truth" energized the group to search for the appropriate question or statement that might be incriminating. "We can strengthen our drama," O'Neill (1991b) argues, "by exploiting the tensions between appearance and reality" (38). Brenda, whether consciously or not, was highlighting how complex reconstructing a historical event can be when the source of that reconstruction is potentially contradictory. Using a hot seat as a drama strategy, in which the students were in role as attorneys asking the questions a witness might face under trial, is known as *role-playing within a role*, considered to be "at the heart of all drama" (O'Neill 1995, 144).

"Often in history," I later said to my students, "it seems that we only get to hear the stories of those who bother to write them down." Tom agreed. Women's stories, he felt, were not adequately represented in history, nor were those of the uneducated. The stories untold, Tom apparently was implying, hold elusive currency. I contemplated Tom's thoughts, and I felt the stirring of what Duckworth (1987) describes as, "the having of wonderful ideas."

"In years to come," I suggested, "if the only written record of your seventh-grade class was prepared by two students, would that account be an accurate reflection?" There was unanimous agreement that it would not. Nadia believed that her "viewpoints" and those of her friends might be distorted if someone else was writing about them, particularly if the writer's impressions were not favorable toward them. "I only ask this," I said, "because I suddenly started to think about the accused soldiers. We don't hear much about their story of the Boston Massacre." My mind was racing with images: soldiers' thought processes, pictures of soldiers in prison, soldiers embittered and angry. "I wonder what happened to them after the shootings?"

Tom knew. They were, he said, "taken to Queen Street in the new jail and kept in prison until October." He was helping to shape a culminating activity in our process drama.

We discussed what the conditions might have been like sitting in an eighteenth-century jail for eight months while waiting for a trial: *dirty, humid,* and *rat-infested* were popular descriptions. "The soldiers' memories of those March 5 events perhaps were their only company," I suggested. "They perhaps constantly thought about the shootings: at morning, during mealtimes, in their dreams." Dreams! Dreams, I thought, capture one's hopes and fears, encapsulate wants and needs. Dreams can be abstract or realistic. They seemed an ideal way of capturing an untold story of history.

The students, in small groups, reflected upon a possible recurring dream an imprisoned soldier might have. These were then enacted. "Sometimes we don't remember our whole dreams," I reflected as the groups began to act them out, "we perhaps can only recall their vague elements or qualities." After each dream was shared, the spectators, in role as the soldiers who had those dreams, recalled them. "Last night I had a dream," Nadia began, "and it was about all these colonists coming toward me." In her dream, she could not escape from her tormentors. "They started running," she continued, "and they stabbed me."

"Did you shoot them?" Teddy asked, in role as a fellow imprisoned soldier.

"I started to," Nadia recalled, "but I missed and they kept coming toward me". Nadia had been describing the improvised dream of Susan, Madelene, and Selene.

Other soldier's dreams had similar claustrophobic qualities. "I had this nightmare," Madelene began, recounting the work of Albert, Tom, and Teddy, "that I was standing in front of two colonists." She had visions of terror. "They were coming closer to me and pointing their guns," she nervously recalled, "and suddenly I lost my gun and they were on top of me and were going to shoot me." She contemplated what that dream meant: "I'm scared that the dead colonists, or some that got injured, might take revenge." I asked her whether she was concerned about this dream. "Yes," she began, "I'm afraid that in court I'll be found guilty."

Although history does not tell us if the soldiers had the dreams we enacted, the activity was a strong one for reflecting on the soldiers' fears and their humanity. We had touched upon an untold and unknown story. A powerful form of reflection, Bolton (1979) argues, is that which occurs at the same time as the drama: "that is from within the drama, so that as things are happening, and as words are spoken, their implications and applications can be articulated legitimately as part of the drama itself" (127). The power of the experience might have been lessened if we routinely discussed the dreams after they were shared. The immediacy of the in-role telling conveyed a sense of the outcasts' suffering and endurance.

The Value of Writing

This view seemed strengthened in light of the students' journal entries, written in the role of imprisoned soldiers. Some of these entries bordered on the poetic. "I have felt the anger and terror that the colonists provoked," Susan began. "I have thought about it over and over, never knowing why that first shot rang out into the cold, hateful air of that night." Remaining in Boston, she concludes, "will not be easy for I feel revenge in the air." The desire to continue living when faced with such constraints and foreboding, Albert ominously concludes, slowly fades. Thoughts of suicide were frequent in his soldier's account:

I'm in great and horrible pain. Sorrow settles in the pit of my heart. My anger rocks my very brain. Life's meaning has been lost through the past few months. We are in enemy camp, prisoners of a deadly war, one which we are in an obvious disadvantage cause Mother Britain knows not of the colonies' rebellious attitude. We are the beginning casuelties, framed by the sly acts of this dirt-infested Boston. It ridicules mother Britain's Boston. The cells here are papered with grime and slime and dirt. They care not for us, but feed us their leftovers. Fellow soldiers are not well either. My long pal attacked me the other day with his teeth and the anger of raby dog. Two young soldiers lay in the corner moaning, claiming headaches and stomach pains. My sane consciousness suppresses all thoughts of rebellions, since trials are coming up and surprisingly, I feel excitement and tingles all over. Life goes on, but temptations to end my life come very often.

It is hard to deny the emotional quality in the above piece: the committed and active voice, capturing a tale of struggle, fear, and denigration. A soldier's story was beginning to be told.

We are beginning to see how teacher artistry can be supported by the kinds of tasks participants are asked to perform, such as the writing students do both in and out of role. Albert, in particular, is a fine example of how a student's writing can help create context and shape perspectives. He once shared his own thoughts on how writing might serve a process drama. "After acting out something," he wrote in his journal, "a person is normally flustered and energetic. An object in motion tends to stay in motion. Writing will allow them to interpret the action in words and this might help them think." Writing, he seemed to imply, provides an opportunity for participants to approach and contemplate the work in a different manner. He appears to value the written mode as a significant expression of the "acting out" experience.

The students had written an array of items, including a diary entry of a Boston patriot, soldiers' letters, cryptic political messages, and counselors' briefing notes. Often these were written through the guise of role, although not always. In each instance, however, the writing seemed to provide a useful forum wherein the students could reflect upon the work, build belief in their roles, and suggest possibilities for future actions. This forum might have involved the students reading their entries aloud before an activity, or perhaps quietly contemplating the work in their journals.

The fact that this writing was not being formally assessed also appeared to be liberating for some students. "I get frustrated," Tom said, describing how he feels when written work was frequently graded in this school. Sometimes he did not "know what to write" because he was so concerned about how the piece would be evaluated. He felt, however, more relaxed about the writing assignments we had engaged in. Describing his own writing processes, he said, "I just kind of go with the flow."

The opening and closing sentences of his letter to Captain Preston, for example, characterizes this liberal and energetic spirit. Tom begins his letter with a desperate appeal, "Capt., Capt., you have got to tell me what happened in your trial. Pound for pound excitement fills my heart of fear and confusion, because of the long awaited trial." This tone contrasts with the exhausted voice of closure, "Every second I think of that second as my last breath of life. Ugh, I feel an acuteness of pain flowing through my bones." I have quoted numerous other examples in this chapter where the students' writing seems to "go with the flow."

Furthermore, Tom conceded that he had a greater sense of being fulfilled as a writer when he wrote during the drama. "I enjoy it more because I don't really have to worry about what's at hand." There may be an important lesson here for teachers who hope to break down the negative attitudes students sometimes have toward writing in social studies. If, as Berthoff (1981) argues, imagination helps form perception, and if students "learn to write" through means of "playing" and "working" with language and "using it instrumentally," then perhaps greater attention should be given to the writing possibilities promoted by process drama in the social studies classroom.

The Dynamics of Small-Group Work

Similarly, the artistry here is tied into gaining participants' commitment to dramatic action through their small-group work and the sense of ownership that it generates. Little attention has been given in the literature to the manner in which small groups function in a process drama—how they reach their decisions and how participants negotiate in them. Earlier, for example, I commented on how Brenda, Selene, Amara, and Joyce seemed to work effectively as a group when preparing their victimization scene. The quality of their work appeared connected to the dynamics operating in their small group: mutual support and trust.

This quality was not a characteristic of all the small-group work. Meryl, Nadia, Tom, and Albert, for example, working on the same task as the four girls, had faced what seemed to be insurmountable dynamics as they attempted to make a decision.

MERYL: What are we going to do?
NADIA: I think we should do rumors.
TOM: What do you want to do that for?
MERYL: I vote rumors.
TOM [Grudgingly]: All right, rumors.
MERYL: What rumor should it be?
TOM: Just whisper it in your ear.
NADIA: We should make a rumor about Tom!
MERYL: And a girl.
NADIA: No, a boy! Let's make a rumor about Tom.
MERYL: What shall we say?

NADIA: Yesterday wasn't really his birthday. He was fakin'.

TOM [Noting her ring]: Why do you wear that ring?

MERYL: What?

NADIA: It's cute.

ALBERT: No, it's not.

NADIA: It is.

TOM: It has white and red.

MERYL: It's the style.

NADIA [Angry]: I didn't say anything about you, so shut up! [Folds her arms, purses lips. Silence]

TOM: So why don't you do another style?

MERYL: Oh, let's talk about rumors please. [Nadia refuses to speak, clearly upset]

MERYL: You hurt her feelings.

TOM: Good!

MERYL: Shut up. She didn't say anything.

The apparent dynamics in this group had remained fixed on personal agendas. These students, four of the more outgoing ones, had seemed to block the discussion, focusing on insult and innuendo rather than supporting ideas and actively searching for role possibilities.

This dynamic contrasted markedly with a later moment. In this instance, Albert, Tom, and Teddy were, in their small group, deciding upon a soldier's dream:

TOM: Maybe we could just do a re-enactment of the massacre.

TEDDY: No, let's make up our own nightmare.

TOM: Let us change it a little bit.

TEDDY [Sarcastically]: Yea, right. Let the colonists shoot, right!

TOM: Yea. That would be perfect.

ALBERT: Okay, a soldier was shooting right . . . then suddenly a colonist raised their guns.

TEDDY: No, the soldiers are really holding a stick, and then the colonists like switch weapons.

ALBERT: We've gotta show like that the soldiers are being oppressed.

TOM: No, we gonna do this right. Just at the moment when they're about to fire they will say "Oh, where's my gun?" and then the colonists, right, will laugh "Ha. Ha. Ha!" and pull out their guns and aim their guns at the person and it doesn't shoot.

TEDDY: No, it shoots.

TOM: And then the soldier like wakes up.

TEDDY: Who's sleeping? We need four persons.

TOM: Two colonists and one soldier.

ALBERT [to Teddy]: And then you go bang and then he falls down and you're asleep.

TOM: Okay.

The three boys, working more comfortably as a group, were able to listen to each suggestion, using the ideas as a step closer to deciding upon their dream. Each voice appeared to have equal status and, more important, was respected. There did not seem to be any personal motive other than that of generating task possibilities and supporting peer contributions.

Small-group work, therefore, can be an exciting forum for building ideas and commitment to dramatic action, but sometimes the dynamics operating in the group can thwart the work's development. Teachers need to be alert to these dynamics if they are interested in developing process dramas in their classrooms.

Teacher-in-Role

Finally, artistry is tied into the teacher's or leader's ability to step into role, a strategy widely referred to as *teacher-in-role*. Although this strategy has been criticized, primarily because of its misconstrued manipulative connotations (see Faulkes-Jendyk 1975; Hornbrook 1989), it appeared to help these students find a voice for themselves in the drama. The students suggested that there were two reasons for this voice. The first had to do with the teacher as cocreator, and the second dealt with the manner in which the strategy helped create an artistic framework.

When the teacher assumes a role, "it makes you want to participate," Nadia confided during an interview. "It shows," she continued, "that you're involved with everybody." When I asked her how it might have been different if I were not playing a role, she elaborated, "It would be like you were just standing there watching over us in your head correcting what we're doing and everything but if you're with us and you mess up nobody's going to correct you." She seemed to be implying something about the nature of risk taking. If the teacher is playing along with the group rather than being the chief critic of their work, it can encourage the students to participate in the play and take risks too.

From my observations and interactions with these students, it appeared that this teacher posture of joining in and negotiating with a class was not frequently encountered in their school. One further element that surprised them about my own teaching style was my unconventional approach in the classroom. "You're so goofy," Tom jokingly said of me during an interview. "It just never seems like you're a teacher," Nadia concurred. "It seems like you're just one of us and we're just talking." Noticing my interest in her statement, she provided an example, "Like when you sit on your chair and you sit on your legs." Teachers, apparently, did not typically sit on their legs in this school. "I think it's better that way," Nadia continued, "than having a big stiff teacher standing in front of you."

Apparently, because I was signaling a more equal status, this posture transformed the classroom environment from being typically hierarchical, formal, and product-oriented to a more laissez-faire and equitable one. Interestingly enough, Nadia also cited "humor" as a frequent quality of classroom discourse that contributed toward the relaxed atmosphere. Teacher role-play, therefore, may need to be coupled with a personality that encourages student participation.

Another important feature of the teacher-in-role that the students mentioned was its story-creating ability, what I liken to its artistic purpose. "When you are in it," Susan said, "we can think of more things." Meryl agreed: "People get more understanding and can participate." It helps create an atmosphere, Teddy suggested. The support of the teacher's role-playing was helping the students, as Susan said, "get more ideas." This is quite different from telling the group what their ideas should be. "My belief in my attitudes," Heathcote (1971) once said, "supports [the students'] beliefs in theirs, but this type of teaching takes courage at first and it is always a calculated risk" (51). I think it is a misreading to view teacher role-play as a subversive manipulation. It might be helpful to remind ourselves that just as artists are manipulating forms when rendering artworks, so the teacher-in-role is an artist who renders dramatic meaning.

But such rendering does not always lead to satisfying artistic experiences. I had read excitement in the group when I assumed the role of the mystery host, but I did not read excitement when I assumed the role of the supervisor. The circumstances in which both these role-plays took place were characteristically different:

There were varying levels of engagement, interest, understanding, and experience. It might well be that the more familiarity the students have of the technique will influence their degree of investment in it. At the same time, however, if there is no dramatic hook, as Bolton (1984) says, that can draw the students into the work, group familiarity with the technique may have negligible impact.

Learning through process drama requires a leader's ability to assume roles and personae that can probe the selected curriculum issues. Such learning, contrary to what some critics say, responds to the creative impulse of an artist, rather than to the technical concerns of the craftsperson. "The craftsperson uses skills to achieve a predetermined end," writes O'Neill (1995), "but the artist uses skills to discover ends through action" (64). As we have seen, the process drama worker is geared towards discovery rather than to finding solutions. The teacher-in-role, then, is an artist who can demonstrate to the students the kinds of decisions they are working toward, the kinds of outcomes these might have, and the sorts of consequences their decisions could entail.

The teacher-in-role is not an actor playing a scripted part, but a type of artistic pedagogue who can push the group into new ways of thinking and new kinds of feeling. The teacher-in-role strategy can be one of the most powerful tools available to process drama leaders searching for ways to press the group in its quest for meaning and clarity. When teachers work alongside the group in role they are able to shape and contribute to the dramatic work from within the art form.

But as with any artistic endeavor the leader requires special qualities, such as, "the toleration of anxiety and ambiguity, as well as a willingness to take risks and court mystery and the courage to confront disappointment and, on occasion, the possibility of failure" (O'Neill 1995, 65). The strategy can potentially open up many of the rich knowledge possibilities available to leaders concerned with learning through process drama.

4

Building a Knowledge Base
Learning About
Process Drama

I was keen to know what the students had been learning about the work we had experienced. While they had clearly learned through the process drama, and in it, what would they say about the quality of the experience, and, how might they demonstrate that quality to me and to each other? "We have an experience," Dewey reminds us, "when the material experienced runs its course to fulfillment" (1934, 35). In traditional classrooms, however, it tends to be the teacher who decides what constitutes educational "fulfillment." Rarely are students engaged as active collaborators in this process. Some social studies educators have argued against such collaboration on the basis that students should be instructed "to learn . . . content" only (Parker 1991, 92). Unfortunately, notions of "fulfillment" are, in these instances, construed in terms of a chapter test or other written evaluation forms that demand "the regurgitation of information already gathered" (Parker 1991, 89). A formal written test, I thought, would tell me little about what the group had learned about our process drama.

It would have undermined the collaborative spirit of the drama to impose such a formal measuring tool; such would have been an inappropriate measure for celebrating fulfillment. Answering twenty multiple-choice questions on propositions related to the Boston Massacre, for example, would not indicate what the experience of participating in the process drama meant to the students, even though such testing had earlier been the predominant means through which they had described success or failure in social studies. How would the seventh graders now characterize fulfillment in the process drama?

"It seems that we've just about finished," I casually mentioned to the group, "but have we finished?" My contemplations on whether or not our experience of process drama had "run its course" led Albert to claim that the work, for him, was incomplete. Others agreed, implying that closure had not satisfactorily been reached.

"All of our work seemed to begin," I reflected, "when the Superdupervisor came across an ancient document written by a William LeBaron." We reminisced over all the different activities we had engaged in since that discovery: the formative moments from LeBaron's life; a Tory/Whig chase; the journey through Boston's streets; the meeting with a stranger; the preparations for a legal defense, and so on. "When did we stop being People of the Future?" Nadia asked. A good question. I could not remember. I asked, "Did we ever stop being those people?" Tom thought not. He maintained that when we entered the time capsule and returned to eighteenth-century Boston, we were role-playing visitors from a future time. Returning to the context of future people could be a useful medium for culminating our experience of process drama.

"If we accept Tom's statement," I casually proposed, "I wonder how those supervisors might share their experience with other future people when they came back from Boston?" I was hoping here that if the group could project themselves into the role of supervisors who had to report on their encounter, it might more immediately help them identify what the experience of process drama holds for them. We canvassed a range of reporting possibilities, including creating a report to the Superdupervisor; privately informing family members; creating a newspaper; writing a book; having an artist draw important moments; or possibly making a film. Our discussion then turned to the merits of each of these storytelling devices.

"Books turn yellow," Tom declared, discounting this idea as a viable possibility. "Besides," he continued, "what about people who don't understand that language?" Jessica liked the idea of a book. "Those who could read," she argued with Tom, "could tell those who couldn't." Tom, Meryl, and Albert preferred a film, believing this would reach more people. "What if the audience were blind?" retorted Nadia, "what if they were deaf?" Meryl, attempting some kind of a compromise, suggested that "sometimes there are books that go with movies."

While the students were dialoguing between themselves on what might constitute an effective strategy for sharing the supervisors' Boston experience, I asked which one, if any, was more appealing. A heated disagreement ensued between those arguing for a book and those proposing a film. "Let those who want to do the book, do it," concluded Nadia, "and those who want to do a film, do that." This seemed acceptable to the whole class. They divided into three groups: two focused on film making and one on writing a book.

As they enthusiastically set to task on their various assignments, I noted how they were making their own decisions: Subjects and groupings were their choice. Unlike in earlier work, my role seemed less of a leader and more of a facilitator or a supporter of classroom discourse. Freire (1970) argues that only when teachers engage in "authentic" dialogue with their students will they later become self-reliant and assume responsibility for their education. Such is achieved when

the teacher-of-the-students and the students-of-the-teacher cease to exist and a new term emerges: teacher-student with student-teacher. The teacher is no longer merely the one-who-teaches, but one who is himself taught in dialogue with the students, who in their turn, while being taught, also teach. (67)

I sat and watched as the students appeared to be assuming the roles of reflective practitioners as they planned, reflected, and acted upon their group's decision making. The learning tasks were now primarily the responsibility of the students themselves. How could I have predicted before this task that the students would decide on a film and a book as the means through which they would communicate the supervisors' experience of the Boston Massacre? How would I have known that they would embark upon these projects in such a committed way? How do teachers accommodate the individual and group meanings that students bring to a classroom event? How does process drama accommodate a multiplicity of interests, attitudes, agendas?

It seems that there are no simple solutions to structuring process drama. Given the unpredictability of classroom interactions, it is important that lesson plans have a flexible framework, which will provide many entry points for groups to encounter the work. To prevent Nadia, Jessica, and Teddy from writing a book, on the basis that the majority of their peers were interested in making a film, would have undermined the concept of educational fulfillment. Learning about process drama then requires leaders to search for the appropriate vehicle or device in which participants can demonstrate their relationship to the work and what the experience of participation has meant for them. Overall, learning about process drama involves:

- understanding how to operate the dramatic art form
- having participants act as collaborators and in a collegial manner
- recognizing the art form's power to reveal and probe human nature
- developing critical skills when observing, and responding to, others' work
- being informed about what leads to satisfying work
- celebrating individual and group achievement

RECOUNTING THE PROCESS DRAMA EXPERIENCE

It now seems appropriate to describe the students' chosen methods of recounting their process drama experience in social studies—that is, the means through which they decided to honor their own work, within the context of their identity as reflective practitioners, and what they seemed to be learning about process drama. In describing the means through which the students demonstrated their understanding, I have categorized their group learnings around three key themes: (1) process drama can be confronting and self-revelatory; (2) process drama is hard work; and (3) process drama requires collaborative artistry.

Process Drama Can Be Confronting and Self-revelatory

"While we're doing the glitter," Susan dictated to Madelene, "Joyce steps into the time machine." Susan was describing how she felt her group's film should begin. This film was going to recreate the journey back to Boston through the eyes of Joyce, a time traveler. "No, that would take too long," Madelene insisted, "the camera will pick up Joyce preparing." The problem was, it seemed, the question of whether or not there would be sufficient glitter, a prop used to suggest a flashback, to enable Joyce to set up for the next scene. Susan clearly thought there would be.

This group's film was developing into a high-tech production. The emphasis on stage properties seemed particularly important. Susan delegated these responsibilities: Bells were required to recapture the signals for fire during the Boston Massacre; guns for the soldiers were needed; a judge's cloak and gavel had to be found for the trial; and a book must be located to represent a Bible. Joyce was evidently able to bring in to class a toy gun. "Does it have like a real gun noise?" inquired Susan, hoping to recreate a realistic effect for the King Street shootings, "or does it sound silly?" I could detect some tension when Madelene retorted, "Susan, we're not allowed to bring guns into school." Madelene was slowly developing antagonism toward Susan's monopoly on all the decisions.

"Mr. Taylor," called Susan. I gingerly walked over to the group from the side of the room, expecting to be asked for an adjudication. "We were just discussing, you know, the Boston Massacre," she said. "They had guns, and we were just wondering if we can bring guns in, for when you shoot our film." I recalled how the principal had put a ban on any items coming into the school that dealt with or suggested guns in any form. This included magazines, pictures, and, unfortunately, toy guns. Although they seemed disappointed when I advised that it probably went against school policy, the girls willingly considered other alternatives. But when their film was videotaped in a later session, I learned that they had ignored my advice. Joyce had brought in her toy guns.

Their film was taking shape. "I am to step into a time machine," wrote Joyce in her journal, describing its framework. "When I step out of it, I'm in Boston in 1770 and also in the middle of a patriot's meeting." They were going to arrange the lockers into the shape of a time machine. The Molineux meeting house would be suggested by a table. "The patriots are sitting at the meeting very still," Joyce continued. "Once I clap my hands together and sit down they began to argue about what to do about the soldiers." It was interesting how a hand clap would signal that scene's beginning. Although the group had not formally discussed the conventions of film making, they had decided on an economical and clear device for launching the work.

"After the meeting everybody goes home," wrote Joyce. "The bells began to ring and the patriots went out to King Street. Some got shot at by the soldiers." Her group would try to recreate the

Boston Massacre, with Selene and Brenda role-playing the soldiers. The next scene would focus on the trial, and then Joyce would return "back to the future and finish her journal."

It was a tight framework, neatly balanced with Joyce writing in her log at the film's beginning and end. Joyce would be assuming a prominent role in the work. While I watched with interest how eagerly she improvised Susan's directions, my attention was drawn to a showdown that was apparently looming between Madelene and the self-proclaimed director: The following dialogue took place right after the group had finished reconstructing the King Street shooting.

SUSAN : Okay, let's do the court now.

MADELENE [Role-playing the judge. Mockingly]: Where do I sit?

SUSAN [Directs her to a desk]: Make sure you wear the cloak correctly!

SUSAN [To Joyce]: You're the witness, and you two [pointing to Selene and Brenda], are the visiting counsellors. Now move your seats, okay.

SUSAN [Assuming the role of John Adams]: And now for my final witness, I call Joyce. Joyce, on that day what did you see?

JOYCE [Loudly. Confidently]: I saw boys around the soldiers and the soldiers smacked them.

SUSAN [Out of role]: Oh, you need a Bible to swear your oath, you haven't sworn your oath. [Grabs a Bible. Joyce swears oath. Susan again role-plays Adams] Okay, on that day what did you see?

JOYCE: Well, I was coming out because I thought there was a fire right, and just saw like there was just one soldier. Then, there were all these boys and they were like harassing them.

Susan then reminded Madelene to inform the lawyers to ask questions. Madelene wasn't sure what Susan expected.

SUSAN: Ask them! Ask Brenda and Selene, "How do you plead?"

MADELENE [Hostile look. Mechanically]: "How do you plead?" [Silence]

SUSAN [Angry] : You guys are supposed to say, "Not guilty." But first you [Madelene] say to her [Joyce] that you can leave the stand. That's before you [Madelene] say to them [Brenda and

Selene], "How do you plead?" Okay? Then you [Madelene] say
that one of them is guilty and one is not. . . . Let's do it again.

The demands of small-group negotiation can be great. Does the
teacher protect students from experiencing these demands? "Children must work for autonomy," Bolton (1985b) claims, "they must
find resources within themselves to earn power" (154). Dealing
with and accommodating a variety of different ideas can be a struggle. These students were learning that process drama demands collegial relationships and the ability to negotiate fairly and compromise when necessary.

Madelene appeared frustrated by Susan's insistent directions.
However, if teachers are, as Grundy (1987) argues, "serious about
the power of the learner to control the learning situation, then it
follows that the power to engage or not in the learning situation
should reside with the learner" (127). It was evident that Susan was
not simply going to hand the responsibility of director to Madelene
unless Madelene made a bid for it. These students were being
reminded that encounters with process drama can be confronta-
tional and self-revealing.

Eventually, Madelene did resist Susan. This conflict occurred
immediately before they were going to be videotaped. "They've
changed everything," Susan cried as I walked into the room with
the camera. Apparently, there had been a major altercation minutes before. The five of them were sulking by the wall. "Maybe I
should have intervened earlier," I reflected in my log that evening,
"but sometimes kids just have to learn how to work with each other
by themselves. They can't always have an adult showing the way and
cushioning them from upsetting confrontations." Despite these
tensions, the film went ahead. Ironically, Madelene later wrote in
her journal how she enjoyed working "with each other" in the small
group. Susan too reflected on "the fun and thinking I had and
did." I wondered what that thinking entailed.

Seventh graders, I contemplated after this incident, are resilient
and complex: friends one minute, arch enemies the next; passive in
one class, domineering in another. Although Susan was dictatorial
in the role of director, it was intriguing to note this posture that
was so uncharacteristic of her. This was one of the few times in the
process drama when she indicated such a commanding presence.
"Some people have changed through all this study of Boston,"
Selene wrote, "they are learning that they can talk in front of the

class if they knew that everyone was a friend." While she does not go into further detail, perhaps she was identifying the possible transformation in Susan.

When Brenda reviewed a video of her group planning their movie, she also hinted that there was a qualitative difference in their approach to educational tasks:

> They're ready for work and are proud of what they're doing. It shows me a lot of school spirit and a positive attitude of each and everyone's personality. I'm sure they will keep on working hard and be ready for any challenges that comes in between or through their lifetime.

If, as Heathcote (1990) asserted, there is a connection between students controlling their own choices and their enthusiasm for classroom activities (48), then maybe teachers need to hear the voices of Brenda and her peers with greater vigor. Encouraging students to "realize their power to decide how they might want to design the work" (48) and then facing how those decisions might translate in action, considering volatile group dynamics, appear to be important features of structuring process drama.

Students, like their teachers, need to understand the power of flexibility. When Susan was dictating to her peers how they should act and what they should say in their film, she seemed to be imposing her own sense of fulfillment on the others in her group. We all have different drives, varying needs, and personal views on what constitutes an experience. It appears presumptuous of both teacher and student to predetermine what these may be. If process drama, as O'Neill (1991a) argues, develops most "successfully through the kind of scenic organization which allows both composition and improvisation, exploration and discovery" (5), then it appears crucial to enable participants to negotiate their own agendas honestly and then assume responsibility for their decisions. Often self-revelation can occur only when students become accountable and are confronted to justify their positions.

Process Drama Is Hard Work

While Susan's group was busily devising a film script and rehearsing scenes, Nadia, Teddy, and Jessica were intent upon writing a three-chapter book on the massacre. "I favored the book idea over the film," wrote Jessica in her journal, "because the book was more of a challenging structure." As we approached the time when we would share the projects, however, Jessica reconsidered her choice. "Can we do a film now?" she asked. The demands of the "challenging structure" were becoming more apparent.

One difficulty the group faced was deciding for whom their book was going to be written. "It's not a children's book," Nadia insisted. Apparently a children's book would require artwork, and she did not think they had the time for that. The book, she declared, was going to be pitched at high school students who "knew something" about the massacre, so the book "won't have to go into so much detail." Nadia, it seemed, was not planning to write a long text.

"We're going to explain that it was really a memorable event," she proceeded to inform me. "Shall we do every chapter together or take them separate?" It was really up to them, I explained. I noticed how Nadia assumed responsibility for many of the group's decisions. She would write the first chapter on Boston and "create a scene so that you understand what the place looks like and what's going on." Jessica would then write about the massacre, although "it wasn't really a massacre," but rather an "exaggeration." And Teddy would write the concluding chapter, and he would explain about "the trial and how it ended up."

Teddy offered to type the three chapters up for the group, indicative of his generous spirit. Nadia seemed grateful, although Jessica did not appear concerned either way, and almost seemed bored at times. As it turned out, Jessica would be out of school for the duration of the semester because of illness, and she would not participate in our culminating session.

Eventually they decided on a title for their book, "Our Bostonian Adventure." Teddy had suggested originally, "Back to the Past," but Nadia said she was not happy with the way that title "sounds." Although Nadia had earlier written in her journal that she likes group work because "you learn more," I wondered how receptive she really was to others' ideas. If anything, she seemed to be seeking my assurance that she was progressing satisfactorily.

"How can I get into the fact that I saw this a long time ago?" Nadia proceeded to ask. She was now grappling with narrative sequence. Teddy was not burdened with such questions; he seemed to understand precisely the style and content of what he would write:

We owe our lives to those who won us our freedoms from Great Britain. If those events, the events that gave us, U.S., that happen didn't happen, "probably" we all would be poor and uneducated. I'm not saying that under Great Britains rule is bad, (Well, I can't really tell you if its going to bad, because it didn't happen, I hope it doesn't happen), but I think that we, U.S. Citizens, know that if there was even better government, I think we would stick with our own government.

I admired Teddy's direct candor. In many respects, he seemed more independent than Nadia and Jessica. His decision to be part of the book club appeared more an expression of personal desire and was not governed by what his best friends, Tom and Albert, had chosen. Jessica and Nadia, on the other hand, tended to let peer-group interests influence their choices.

This group seemed to be learning that demonstrating a relationship to the work is hard and demanding, and that achieving easy solutions to complex problems would not be possible. While Nadia and Jessica had perhaps thought that writing the book would involve little time, they were now beginning to regret their decision. However, they had to honor the fact that book writing was their choice and was something they had to see through.

Process Drama Requires Collaborative Artistry

In his journal, Tom described his group work as having "a sense of togetherness . . . I have come to realize and was able to look beyond the film itself. . . . I saw four people working together as a team, maybe even as a family." He seemed to be reflecting on the spirit of comradeship that characterized the working process in his group. Unlike the tensions encountered by the other filmmakers, Tom, Meryl, Albert, and Amara were more casual and lighthearted in their approach, joking and laughing, yet still, as Albert claimed, productive, "which not only lightens the atmosphere but shows that they can do the work with ease."

The painstaking property lists, so prominent with the other film group, were unimportant here. These filmmakers were more interested in workshopping possible actions than in external trappings. My log captured their rehearsal process in its early phases:

> While Albert, like Susan, has taken the initiative, there seems to be more opportunities for the others to throw ideas into the center for discussion. Tom leans over Albert's shoulder and suggests that they create a time capsule. Albert agrees, writing it down.

Quickly they get up and start fashioning a mock set. Tom, Meryl
and Amara stand in a tight circle facing outward. Albert instructs
them to lean back to convey a sense of propulsion through
time. Tom doesn't like the idea of three time travelers. They now
change it. Meryl and Amara become the time travelers. Desks
are to be packed in together to suggest the machine, and the girls
will crawl out of these.

Meryl decided that an audience would only understand what was
happening if they had a narrator. Albert volunteered for this role,
preferring not to act in the film. Meryl compared their teamwork
to Niagara Falls: "Look at the Niagara falls. It's a lot of little drops
of water working together as a team." She would later comment on
the changes that had taken place in some people: "we have grown
confidence + their for feel comfortable to participate in class. I
think some people have crawled out of their shell."

Amara, for instance, described how "more comfortable and
relaxed" she felt. She reflected on her group's ability to "not argue
with their classmates." Individuals, she contends, were able, "to be
part of the group and not be let out or alone and could relate and
adapt with the people that they used to don't feel comfortable
with." Amara would role-play a time traveler, patriot, and soldier in
their film. The rehearsal process was riveting to watch.

Tom suggested how she might walk through the alleyway, a cluttered arrangement of desks, on the way to Molineux's house. She
must, he asserted, look back over her shoulder "suspiciously." She
eagerly followed the direction. Albert, too, watched with interest
and later wrote in his journal, "Amara, who I think used to be very
shy, seem very brave now." He, also, had noticed a change in her.
Although Albert was still not happy with the alleyway effect because
he wanted to "push the desks in closer," he implied that this detail
seemed less important than people's "changes in shyness."

"In the beginning," wrote Amara about the film, "me and Meryl
are traveling within a time capsule to the 1700s to William Moli-
neix's meeting through roads and alleys." Albert suggested a possible narrative: "The two future people are encased within a fourth
dimensional intinerant conveyance, or known in the 20th century
as a time machine." The group liked this link and encouraged him
to develop it more. Albert, although enjoying this responsibility,
seemed to depend on his peers' suggestions while the narrative of
the time travelers was constructed. He wrote:

They have a mission, to experience 3 situations in the 1700s near the event of "The Boston Massacre." They work for a Superdupervisor, the big honcho and the main cheese. He was the first who presented to them subjects involving the "Boston Massacre."

In a future session, he brought in a flashlight that would suggest "a complicated thingamigig"; in the film it represented a device through which the future people could assume the bodies of eighteenth-century people.

The filmmakers seemed to have an intuitive sense of the form in which they were working. In my mind, it was a complex idea to create with clarity and specificity the idea of future people going back to a treacherous and dangerous time, yet the students did not seem burdened with such thoughts. This ease was most apparent in a concluding scene, set in prison, which Amara described in her journal.

"Meryl is the soldier having the nightmare while sleeping," she wrote. "I am her spirit coming out of her and Tom is a patriot shooting me." How are they going to capture this cogently on film, I wondered? "Then I go back into Meryl and am a soldier sleeping next to her. She then wakes me up and tell me about the nightmare." In effect, Amara would be representing both Meryl's spirit and a fellow soldier.

Film directors might be challenged with the demands of aptly conveying this sequence, but these artists weren't. Albert's clear stage direction left no doubt what was happening: "Meryl sleeps on floor. Amara looms in. Tom comes and shoots her. Amara falls beside Meryl. Meryl wakes up and screams. She informs Amara that she had a nightmare."

It was exciting to watch this group play with their ideas, try them out in action, and then revise them for clarity. "I used to think my work was good," wrote Albert, "but now I see it can be better." He was contemplating the power and support of small-group interaction. I remembered how frustrated he became in earlier work when others would not move at his rapid pace. He now appeared more tolerant and receptive of his peers' ideas. So did Tom.

"I remember when I saw this child, Albert," Tom wrote, "always argueing with this other boy, me, in the 1st couple of weeks." Now it was different. "In the last days I see them working together and sharing our ideas." His thoughts lead him to other observations:

I also saw a certain girl, Madelene, become more active in her schoolwork. When we're working as a group we don't feel lonely or having to face the neglections of others. Therefore, turning all negative thoughts and feelings into positive workmanship. I just had a thought. I know a project can't change someone's life, but did you realize that by studying Boston and Boston Massacre, it showed us that America was able to work together even when they weren't united. Perhaps this project sunk into our heads, and improved our abilities of "working together." You never know.

In the true spirit of reflective practice, the students were reflecting upon their actions as a means for suggesting future ones. They had come a long way and were learning that process drama requires the artful selection of techniques that can best demonstrate their relationship to a given person, subject, or period.

CONCLUSION

After the films had been videotaped and the book written, the whole group assembled to share their projects. The Superdupervisor, the teacher-in-role, welcomed the time travelers, and he explained how interested people of the future would be to hear about their Boston exploits.

This session, he explained, would entail the sharing of work in progress. Unfortunately, he said, one of the supervisors, Jessica, had fallen sick (Jessica was actually ill this day), and she would be unable to participate in this event. The supervisors regretted her absence, and they understood that Jessica's colleagues, who went ahead and prepared a book anyway, would be sharing an incomplete project.

Supervisor Albert introduced his group, and he explained their film's concept. "The Boston Massacre made differences," he suggested, "in the life of a modern nation." That "little upsetting incident" was the "first sign of a yearn from the ever tightening control of Britain." In making the film he was about to share, he hoped to show that "we travel back in time in order to show future men how it is like back then." Although it may "seem boring" to some, for him and his coworkers "this film has historic value." He conceded that the film was only a "condensed version," but perhaps others may be encouraged to "go the videolink and type up files upon files of stuff on the Boston Massacre." The film was then shared.

The supervisors seemed most appreciative of this group's efforts, although some sections of the film were confusing to them. "Why was Meryl wearing that thing on her head?" asked Supervisor Nadia, noticing the covering on Meryl's face when she exited the time capsule. The filmmakers explained that they wanted to create an effect that Meryl was "a future people who looks different from them in Boston." Nadia, on the other hand, particularly liked the manner in which Meryl and Amara were hidden in the time capsule. It created an "atmosphere," she suggested, similar to another film entitled *The Planet of the Apes*, which she had recently seen. We see here how the whole group was developing the skills to appraise critically their own work and that of their peers.

Before the second film was shown, Supervisor Teddy said he thought that the scene of Meryl's nightmare, when she screamed on the ground, was effective. Meryl was disappointed in that moment, however, suggesting that the nightmare would have been more powerful had Amara been "a colonist dressed as a soldier" who fired shots. She also thought their Molineux meeting could have been "better" had they incorporated sound effects. She had seen the other film group's preparations and felt that their use of sound helped generate a sense of "what's going on." Again, the process drama had helped the students develop powerful observation skills and then find the means by which they can make their observations clear to others.

Like Meryl, the supervisors were unanimous with their praise of these effects in the second film. Although Susan expressed concern that the glitter was not all that successful in indicating Joyce's flashback, she did feel the film suggested "what excitement and fear they had when they traveled there." Supervisor Tom proposed, "I think we should put [both films] together." The energy of his own group's film could be coupled with the scenic props and sound effects of Susan's. "I love that," Nadia responded, enthusiastically agreeing with Tom's idea.

It was in this climate of mutual support that the book was read. Nadia passed out the copies. "The book was good even though it was short," Selene later wrote. "I especially liked the designs on the paper and the way they typed the first letter of each chapter." Supervisor Teddy had been diligent, designing an American flag and drawing ferocious-looking bald eagles to adorn the chapters. "I think that going back to Boston," Teddy later wrote in his journal; "is one of the most successful + interesting adventure we ever had because we could learn what happened in the past." The supervisors seemed to agree with Teddy, and they applauded Meryl's earlier suggestion that the book would be an excellent accompaniment for the two films.

Susan had one minor criticism. She thought that it might have been helpful if the book had mentioned something about "benefit of the clergy." We asked her what she meant. When researching her own film, she explained, she had read how Matthew Killroy, one of the soldiers found guilty of manslaughter during the trial, received "benefit of the clergy." It was an old English custom, she said, "which meant that his thumb would have been burnt with a hot iron." It was a punishment. Teddy, like the rest of us, had not heard of this custom before, but he appeared grateful to Susan for the suggestion.

All three projects had now been shared. "What a wonderful, beautiful, way to honor your work, and for you to tell your stories," the Superdupervisor whispered, or was it the teacher? Both seemed genuinely moved. The group, too, seemed satisfied with their efforts. As I blankly looked up, contemplating the silence, a myriad of memories raced through my mind: People of the Future; a mystery document; William LeBaron's life; a game called "Tory and Whig"; secret routes through misty streets; a dead spy; Boston patriots; incriminations; eye-witness accounts. We had traveled a long road. Whole-group drama; small-group talk; teacher-in-role; students in role; using a hot seat; working in pairs; role-playing; map-making; group projects; film-making; book writing. Oh, the immensity of it all. "In this work, drama," Heathcote (1984) once argued, "what we are trying to do is to make ordinary experiences significant, and that's a hard thing" (24). But teaching in general seems a hard thing, as all the classroom participants seemed to discover at this and other moments as they negotiated and collaborated, shared and listened, improvised and directed. We were learning what makes up process drama and the possibilities of learning about, through, and in it.

I did not know whether I was in or out of the Superdupervisor's role when I finally muttered, "I had no idea where this might take us, this Boston Massacre, you know." But it *had* taken us. It had taken me. "What an event." I was stumbling through my words, not really knowing what I wanted to say. I realized that the meeting had ended: the process drama, I thought, had been consummated; it had come to its fulfillment. Nobody said anything. "Any comments?" I stupidly asked, breaking the silence. There was a pause. Teddy raised his hand. I was hoping he might relieve me of the pressing burden, I foolishly felt, of summing up what these wonderful sessions had meant. Maybe, I thought, he'll encapsulate the complex journey we'd been on. Offer a few words, please Teddy, that could highlight a feeling, or an understanding, that resonates with all of us. "Can I go and have a drink of water before our English test?" he asked. I could not tell whether my raucous laughter was contagious.

So with those words, we were jolted back to the real world of school, with its papers and assignments, teachers and students. We collected our books, arranged the room back to its ugly rows of desks, and wandered off to our different duties. If we wanted to wallow in remorse that our work had ended we could not; there was no time. There were tests to attend to, classes to be taught, grades to be had. On leaving that hot and sticky room on a day in June, I felt that we did so with a sense of satisfaction. We had consummated our experience of process drama and by doing so discovered something about its power to transform people and their behavior.

5

Reflective-Practitioner Research

Throughout this book readers have read a lot about the power of reflective practice to help teachers and their students have informative and challenging encounters with process drama. The improvisational and spontaneous nature of process drama demands that teachers develop the skill to reflect in and on practice; indeed, without the ability to reflect and press self-monitoring steps into their work, leaders would not be able to structure a successful drama experience. It seems to me that reflective practice and process drama go hand in hand. Both are practically oriented since teachers monitor, evaluate, and revise their own practice continuously; they both require open-mindedness and flexibility; and both demand a willingness for leaders to surrender their own agendas and allow the work itself to dictate the terms. In this chapter, I plan to look more closely at what reflective practice is, how it might be conducted, and the benefits of reflective practice for leaders as they begin and continue to implement process drama in their curriculum.

TEACHER RESEARCH AND RELATED MOVEMENTS

There has been a long and healthy tradition of investigative paradigms that support the teacher research I have described in this book. Teacher research, a movement inspired by the late Lawrence Stenhouse (1975), wrested on the conviction that all teaching ought to be based on critical inquiry; that in order for teachers to improve the quality of their work, they should subject it to intensive and focused exploration. Curriculum development should involve teachers directly in the process of evaluating the effectiveness or ineffectiveness of their teaching.

This movement, in many respects, was at odds with a dominating mainstream approach to research, which emphasized clinical and scientific experiments as the only legitimate manner in which research could be conducted. The major tenets of this mainstream quantitative focus include an emphasis on statistical measurement, a need to quantify outcomes, the claims for objectivity and value freedom (or the need for neutral observers). Teacher research, however, operated from a different orientation and posed a contrasting challenge. Teacher research claimed that within educational contexts it is the practitioners themselves who should be the beneficiaries of studies conducted; educational research that did not promote and honor the voices of those in the field—the teachers and their students—and that did not directly influence classroom practice, would have no legitimacy.

Elliot Eisner, a longtime critic of conventional research approaches, has argued that universities have too often conducted "educational commando raids" on schools, when professors and their assistants enter classrooms for the briefest periods only to collect the data quickly and then leave (Eisner 1985, 104, 260). "I am not optimistic," declared Eisner, "about the putative benefits of tightly conducted experiments; classrooms are complex places, and well-controlled experiments have little ecological validity." He regrets the way most educational researchers have "distanced" themselves from the realities of school. "Educational practice as it occurs in schools is an inordinately complicated affair," he argues, "filled with contingencies that are extremely difficult to predict, let alone control." As you have seen, the unpredictability of process drama was a recurring theme in my process drama work. It would have been impossible to predetermine the outcomes, to state the end points, to quantify the learning. Process drama defies the mainstream urge to rationalize, to control, to seek uniformity. The ephemerality and transitory nature of process drama then raises concerns about how we research or investigate an event that is constantly evolving and transforming.

These concerns are also those of the action-research movement, a movement that began in the United States in the early 1940s and aimed to render the problematic social world understandable as well as to improve the quality of life in social settings. The intention of action research was to improve, and hopefully solve, the pressing daily problems that practitioners faced. McKernan (1996) elaborates:

> Action research is carried out by practitioners seeking to improve their understanding of events, situations and problems so as to increase the effectiveness of their practice. . . . [It] aims at feeding the practical judgment of actors in problematic situations. The validity of the concepts, models and results it generates depends not so much on scientific tests of truth as on their utility in helping practitioners to act more effectively, skillfully and intelligently. Theories are not validated independently of practice and then applied to curriculum; rather they are validated through practice. Action research is thus grounded curriculum theory. (3–4)

There is an attractiveness in this description of action research for those of us interested in process drama and how best to document it.[1] Just as process drama revolves around three interconnected processes of planning, implementing, and reflecting, so does action research; the aim of both is to work toward trial and improvement. In placing control over classroom practice and theory in the hands of the practitioner, action research has become a kind of political act that releases teachers into believing in their own capacity to effect change, and to develop confidence in their own ability to act as authoritative leaders in their classrooms. Such a belief is at odds with the mainstream desire to direct outcome and attainment, to develop national standards and uniform exit statements, but it speaks powerfully to the concerns of the process drama worker.

Another related strand to teacher research, one that focuses on the character of reflective action, has been that informed by John Dewey earlier in the twentieth century, and by Donald Schön (1992) in the latter half of the century. Both contrasted routine action with reflective practice; Schön required moving beyond the habitual and commonsense to action characterized by self-appraisal, flexibility, and artistry. Schön, with his colleague Chris Argyris, has written widely on the disempowerment that practitioners face when forced to exercise someone else's judgment, or when they're expected to implement someone else's program. The trick to professional competence, these authors argue, is when workers can become researchers in the practical context, where they are:

- not dependent on the categories of established theory and technique
- not limited to a deliberation about means that depends on a prior agreement about ends
- not separating thinking from doing
- not bound by the conventional and familiar
- not always checking out with a superior if they are operating correctly[2]

When practitioners fall back onto their own resources and are knowledgeable about the constraints of their own behavior, they are more capable of recognizing what change is needed and how best to implement it. One of the implied criticisms of Heathcote and Bolton is that a generation of dedicated teachers has developed who have usurped their own capacity to reflect on their own action, being more interested in duplicating another's curriculum. I think this criticism would be more appropriately pitched at an educational and political system that expects teachers to recycle or transmit another's educational program; perhaps if teachers had been more encouraged to believe in their own ability to design, implement, and reflect on their practice, they would not feel compelled to repeat, sometimes mindlessly, a process drama that doesn't resonate with the context in which it is experienced.[3]

In this respect, Schön's writing on the importance of reflecting in the process of making—of practitioners being able to know in the action—speaks powerfully to the process drama worker. It is this sense of being caught up in phenomena that strongly dominates these encounters. Leaders with their groups have to work through the encounters based on their reservoir of practical and intuitive knowledge.

When we come to research such an encounter, however, the demands placed on us are challenging, as Schön (1992) observes:

> Reflection-in-action has received surprisingly little research attention. But this is explained by its very nature. It is an ephemeral episode of inquiry that arises momentarily in the midst of a flow

of action and then disappears, giving way to some new event, leaving in its wake, perhaps, a more stable view of the situation. We tend to "wipe it out" as soon as it is over, like the error one makes and quickly forgets on the way to discovering the solution to the problem. (125)

It is my view, though, that if teachers can empower themselves to believe in their own capacity to act as researchers, if they can generate faith in their own ability to observe and reflect critically on their work, then they are capable of effecting change in their own educational settings. While the ephemerality of the episodes that comprise both teacher research and process drama may make it difficult for leaders to interrogate their practice, I have shown here how certain techniques and strategies can be utilized to help us understand the kind of impact teachers are having on our students, and on the quality of learning they are providing for them. In the next section, I'd like to review and clarify what these major techniques and strategies are, and to reassert their indebtedness to the qualitative frame of mind.

REFLECTIVE PRACTICE AND
THE QUALITATIVE MIND

As I have attempted to recapture the work I do in process drama, I have drawn on a long tradition of qualitative inquiry. Readers should be able to infer what I understand by the term *qualitative research* from the content of this book. I have a commitment to representing the process drama in detail. I've included the words and gestures of the students, quoting from their journals, from interviews I've had with them, as well as from observations I've recorded in my own logbook. There is an interest in the narrative frame as I try to digest, synthesize, and report on the work. There is an emphasis on story, on dialogue, on interpretation. The value of individual human voice is foremost—a desire to represent the dilemmas presented and to capture the questions raised for me and my students.

As I try to unfathom the complexity of an episode, I resort to extensive descriptions of the event, but the reader is always aware of my own voice, my own piecing together of the data. This concern with interpretation and narrative puts this teacher research firmly within a tradition of research known as the qualitative. I am not so much concerned with solving a problem, with testing hypotheses, with finding solutions, but rather with the generation of issues, problems, and hypotheses. I have not decided in advance what the content of the scenes the students act will be; but we have created them together based on issues that concern us. In this respect, words such as *scene* and *act*, which connote performance and product, may not be all that appropriate when describing the character of process drama. It is perhaps unsurprising then to find that folks committed to this kind of work have avoided using terms that emphasized product over process. However, one of the pitfalls of such an approach has been the unfortunate conclusion by those critical of process drama that the art form was being devalued. As I have argued throughout this book, just because students are enacting an imagined, unscripted work in process does not mean that they are failing to work in an artistic mode.

There are many books on qualitative research design, so I won't go into this method in any great detail, other than to say that fields such as anthropology and sociology have always been dedicated to research that honors human stories and that probes the complexity and challenge of living on this planet. Readers should be comforted to know that qualitative inquiry is now supported as a legitimate means for researching dynamic educational events, such as those that emerge from an encounter with process drama.[4] I would hope that the battles that some of us have had to face in getting our research valued and supported are long gone.

My commitment to the qualitative mind and its application to research in process drama has been the source of some recent criticism,[5] but as I've written elsewhere (Taylor 1990b, 1995a, 1996, 1997, 1998), I believe the *qualitative* dimension is fundamental to the domain of process drama. Just as the qualitative works through interpretation, through interaction, and just as it raises unsettling questions about who we are and where we're going, so does process drama. Just as the qualitative domain works at reconstructing human lived experience and attempts to recall all the complexity and uncertainty of individual and group endeavor, so does process drama. I know there have been some recent writers who have argued that to set up camps—that is, qualitative versus quantitative—is not helpful, and I would partly agree, but at the same time I cannot find a better term than *qualitative* to describe the ways of knowing that inform process drama.

A quantitative researcher knows what has to be tested and sets up an experiment to conduct the test. Hypotheses are formed, controls are established, comparisons are tracked, statistical analyses are formulated, result sheets are prepared, conclusions are drawn. It is a linear process that emphasizes what happens next, and asks, How much more do we have to do? "Well, we need to interview six people," a quantitative researcher might say, or "we need to conduct twenty-two drama sessions," or "we need to have fourteen boys and fourteen girls represented in the survey." The number of things seen or completed is more important to the quantitative researcher than the quality of that number. Even though qualitative researchers might desire more people to interview, or think that more sessions are required for observation, these needs would emerge from their own analysis of the data, rather than being predetermined in advance.

The qualitative researcher wants to generate themes; the quantitative researcher wants to test propositions. Where the qualitative researcher is interested in probing the moment, in trying to unfathom what motivated a student, the quantitative researcher would rarely deviate from the questions that had been foreshadowed at the beginning of an investigation. Both orientations operate from a completely different perspective of knowing. The quantitative researcher is always working toward some end point and will know when it has been reached; the qualitative researcher is caught up in the process, in the here and now, and may never achieve anticipated goals. In this respect, the qualitative researcher works laterally, and is interested in exploring what is happening now. The quantitative worker thinks in a linear fashion, and is arrested by the question of what will happen next. But those who persist in being consumed by what will happen next need to be reminded that the arts, as Dorothy Heathcote said many times, are revelations of what is occurring in the situated present; the arts are fundamentally human interactive processes, working through symbolic forms.

If we accept that the question What is happening to us now? is central to both the qualitative mind and to the process drama educator, how then do we best research that question?

WHAT IS HAPPENING NOW?

The human construction of the dramatic text is central to the process drama encounter. Individuals and groups are reading, rereading, and sometimes misreading what is taking place around them. When Meryl read my presence in role as a threatening one (see Chapter 3), her reaction was to try to control the threat. Not all students saw the immediate danger. Teddy, for instance, tried to convince me to become part of the conspiracy to curb the redcoats, not realizing that in doing so he had confirmed for me the treacherous nature of his comrades' intentions.

The multiple and shifting voices so fundamental to a process drama, and the here-and-now happening that unfolds around the participants, need to be heard and represented when we come to investigate the work. People's perspectives change in the process drama, as they do in life; passionately held positions can transform on the basis of experience and human interaction; once strongly held viewpoints on the world can be displaced and forgotten. In process drama, we are always, it seems, in a constant state of flux. If we accept Maxine Greene's (1995) position that our lives are narratives in the making, then we could say that in process drama we are enacting those unfolding narratives, narratives constructed by multiple and shifting images of self. Greene writes,

> Neither my self nor my narrative can have, therefore, a single strand. I stand at the crossing point of too many social and cultural forces; and, in any case, I am forever on my way. My identity has to be perceived as multiple, even as I strive towards some coherent notion of what is humane and decent and just. At the same time, amidst this multiplicity, my life project has been to achieve an understanding of teaching, learning, and the many models of education; I have been creating and continue to create a self by means of that project, that mode of gearing in to the world. (1)

An exciting aspect of process drama is that our imagination allows us to project into fictional selves, which too are governed by their own multiple and shifting frames. Even Teddy began to realize that he had offered too much revealing information to me, and, thereby, had exposed his Bostonian comrades to a potential threat. He, in role, recognized that drastic and immediate steps needed to be taken; he had been conned, and he needed to seek retribution. Teddy's fictional self shifted its position as it gained further awareness and understanding. How, I wonder, does our research get at the multiple and shifting self?

The Teacher-Researcher's Logbook

In teacher research, we are forever reminded that it is the teacher's own perceptions and observations that are driving the work. It is the teacher's analyses of the process that both give it life and invite future action. Such analyses do not mean that the teacher fails to incorporate the positions of others when determining appropriate steps, but rather they recognize that the teacher is the one sifting and sorting through the multiple and shifting voices, often shaping the action based on the quality and depth of feedback received from other participants.

It is imperative that the teacher finds a medium where the voices that surround a researched event can be recorded and explored. Logbooks are often the most important record for collecting such data. Here, teacher-researchers can document the work as it is experienced, they can dialogue with themselves about the issues and questions raised, and they can begin to ascertain the major threads and themes that are emerging from it.

In qualitative research, of the kind that I have pursued in this book, logbooks are often considered the principal data-collection instrument because the researcher is put at the center of the investigation. Where quantitative research usually demands that researchers remove themselves from the process of data collection so that the findings are not polluted or tainted by the investigators' values (sometimes referred to as researcher bias), qualitative research demands that the investigators' values and subjectivity are at the study's core.

The logbook, therefore, has assumed high status in the teacher-researcher's journey. Throughout the Boston Massacre drama, I constantly used the logbook both as a record of the work and as a forum for me to search for the themes and issues that were driving it. The logbook is my friendly, and sometimes not-so-friendly, companion; it is where I can communicate with myself about the process drama, and, hopefully, gain some distance from it. It is a place where I can discover what is important to me and what isn't important to me.

The time-consuming nature of having to sit down and enter reflections on teaching is well rewarded by the benefit of achieving clarity and insight into a process drama encounter.[6] As I muse in my logbook about the questions that are raised for me during a process drama, I can consider what strategies and techniques might help illuminate the material in a more compelling manner. I can also share the logbook with critical friends who can read and respond to my observations and let me know whether my analyses are supported by the data that I am including.

Other Perspectives: Student
Journals and Interviews

Beyond the teacher-researcher's logbook, it is important that we begin to access the views and positions of others who surround the researched event. Student journals and interviews, for example, can be incorporated into the teacher's logbook, and can provide yet another perspective on the process drama encounter. Readers will have noted how important it was for me to acknowledge what the students were thinking and feeling about the process drama. The journal provided an opportunity for them to record their thoughts in an ongoing manner. These journals would often become the focus for interviews that I would have with them. We would chat about what the work was meaning, what suggestions the students might have for thematic development, where the dramatic emphases lay, and how they would describe the quality of the experience.

Because students are rarely invited to take an active part in their own learning, and given that they do not expect to be consulted about curriculum planning, teachers might sometimes have to spend considerable time breaking down scholastic conventions and encourage students to rethink the whole dynamic of teaching and learning. This might mean that some teachers have to give up an authoritative position that they value and champion, but one fact that should be clear from the work I've described so far is that process drama requires an ability for teachers to surrender their own voice and prioritize the voices of others.

However, process drama encounters, in and of themselves, tend to demand this rethinking anyway, given that students are often determining the action that should be pursued, which means that they cast the teacher into the role of learner. The best teachers of process drama, it seems to me, feel comfortable with listening to the voices of their students. One of the first lessons I learned from watching Cecily O'Neill work in Columbus all those years ago was that it is okay to express your own vulnerability as a teacher to students; it is okay to tell students that you are unsure how the drama might end and that you were depending on them to help shed some light on an unexpected curve or development in the process drama. Student journals and interviews, in this respect, can be quite powerful illuminators of the perspectives that surround a given moment; and when teachers can illuminate the multiple and shifting perspectives, they begin to air the complex and often competing student voices that bring life to a process drama encounter. The many examples I have provided in this book from student journals is a powerful testament to how these documents can inform and enrich the teaching encounter.

The teacher-researcher is on a hunt to release the students' voices, and is often searching for roles in the process drama that will facilitate this release. It is misguided, though, to want these voices to conform, necessarily, with one another. Difference should be valued and acknowledged; difference, as experienced theatre workers would know anyway, has often been the subject of the most compelling human dramas over time. I am then appealing for a use of student journals and interviews that might be contrary to how they are currently employed in schools. I do not want the journals or interviews to be a place where teachers can correct student output, but where teachers and their students can collaborate and negotiate with one another. I do not want the journals and interviews to be graded for their conformity to a checklist of quantifiable points; I want them to be valued as active contributors to the planning of a curriculum action.

Just as the teacher's logbook is a forum for recognizing what is happening now in the process drama, so should the student journals and interviews be seen as part of the process of layering depth and quality into the immediate experience. The tenet "*Less Is More*" should be a guiding principle in how the journals and interviews are constructed. More data does not necessarily help a group understand what is taking place around them when they contract to a process drama encounter.

Videotapes and Audiotapes

The ephemeral and transitory nature of process drama can be frustrating for the teacher-researcher, in that it is hard to recapture an elusive and transformative art form. This fact alone may be one reason why leaders have avoided documenting their work; it is difficult to recall what happened. This challenge is one that theatre critics face, too, as they try to unfathom the details and qualities of live performance. The critics' reconstruction, like the teacher-researcher's, is made from observations, notes, and access to any other artifact that can help piece together the enacted event.

Electronic methods of data collection, such as video- and audio-taping, can be invaluable for the teacher-researcher. Video, in particular, has been widely used in teacher research to help investigators recall and analyze process drama's decisive features. I am reminded of the many videotapes that have been made of Heathcote's practice,[7] and how significant these have been in the deconstruction of her practice. Because there have been so few professionally created videotapes of competent leaders, it is perhaps unsurprising that the field had developed a dependence on these tapes, especially Heathcote's *Three Looms Waiting,* a B.B.C. documentary that had the effect of transforming the thinking of a generation of drama teachers.

I well recall with excitement an archive of Heathcote's recorded teaching in Ohio in the 1970s, which O'Neill suggested might be a good cataloguing assignment for her Ohio State University class, which I took in the late 1980s. The hours that we students put into watching this raw, unedited footage of Heathcote at work gave us privileged access to one of the most inspiring leaders of process drama.[8] The demand required of having to piece together the sessions' sequencing from the videotape meant that we had to observe closely and repeatedly.

But as important as watching the leadership of others can be, I am challenging teacher-researchers to videotape their own practice, so that they can become more informed of how their own teaching personae influence and shape a process drama encounter. Video provides a very important distancing and reflective quality, where the enacted work can be temporarily held up in time, and viewed over and over again. In this respect, video can be a powerful tool for confirming the trustworthiness of any conclusions a teacher-researcher might want to make.

While I don't want to underestimate the usefulness of electronic methods, we must remember that the angle of the camera lens, again, is providing yet another perspective on the work; one that is not necessarily an accurate picture, but a further record. It is helpful to check out with students and peers whether the observations that teacher-researchers are making from watching the tapes are credible ones. Others, especially those present at the time of the recording, might have a different understanding of the events that seem to be demonstrated on the tape.[9]

SEEKING TRUTH: A FINAL WORD

Process drama workers who believe they are searching for a quantifiable truth in their work are misguided. Just as qualitative researchers acknowledge that perspectives are multiple, shifting, and constantly transforming, so process drama leaders must recognize that no one position holds the truth for all. It is hard for us to think about a singular truth unless we ask whose truth it represents and what position it emerges from. A recent criticism of qualitative research, and its widespread interest in the triangulation (or fixing) of data, is that the drive for conformity and confirmation of perspectives may weaken the unpredictable, the diverse and different. We must be careful that the unique and individual voices of Albert, Meryl, Teddy, Tom, and others like them are preserved and heard. In this respect, it is hard for us in teacher research to talk clearly about validity and credibility because it raises this issue, which critical theorists ask all the time: In whose eyes are we referring to the valid? And the credible? If a viewpoint only has acceptability because it has currency within the mainstream, or because it is widely accepted, it may not be any more truthful than the one lone voice that refuses to participate.

I find it interesting, for example, that quantitative researchers have often argued that their findings are more truthful because they have removed the subjective value. Quantitative researchers pride themselves on their *rigor* and their *system*. Indeed, the characteristics of being rigorous and systematic are considered the great hallmarks of quantitative research. "You must be more systematic in your approach," a quantitative researcher might exclaim. "Demonstrate your rigor at all times, rigorous research is what we want."

Now, in recent times, I haven't found these two characteristics, rigor and system, fundamental to either process drama or to process drama research. Both system and rigor emphasize attributes that are in conflict with the kind of teacher research and reflective practice that I am advocating:

There is an inflexibility and an uncompromising harshness and rigidity implied in the term "rigor" [*and "system"*] that threatens to take us too far from the artfulness, versatility, and sensitivity to meaning and context that mark qualitative works of distinction. It is as if, in our quasi-militaristic zeal to neutralize bias and to defend our projects against threats to validity, we were more pre-occupied with building fortifications against attack than with creating the evocative, true to life, and meaningful portraits, stories, and landscapes of human experience that constitute the best test of rigor in qualitative work. (emphasis added, Sandelowski 1993, 1)

System, for example, refers to an ordered, predetermined plan; a set of principles stringently agreed on; a formal, definite, or established scheme or method. With a systems person, you know what you're getting before you've even experienced it. There are little opportunities for steering away from the straight and narrow, little time for entering the margins of meaning, because the program of research activity has been foretold and pre-scripted. In researching process drama, though, an event characterized by its ephemeral, transitory, and elusive qualities, we cannot look for solace in system. System can deny the unpredictability, the spontaneity, and the improvisational structure so central to our work. Rather than adopting a systems approach we should be looking for characteristics that:

- permit divergence and multiplicity
- tolerate ambiguity
- celebrate individual experience
- demonstrate how process drama operates and can be best managed

A systems approach can impose a formal plan of observation, a plan that is limited by the constrained categories that it formulates. Those who are interested in systematic research tend to focus on outcomes, on proof, and on the result of the inquiry, and don't seem to be so much concerned with what is happening to people when they engage with an artistic event. Yet, as Elliot Eisner (1985) reminds us, knowing the outcome of the game tells us little about how to play the game (141). And what teachers are most interested in is how to play the game of teaching better. The kind of research that systems people produce might not have much influence on what happens in drama classrooms or on how teachers can go about their work.

Neither am I encouraged by those researchers who emphasize rigor as fundamental to drama investigations. *Rigor,* our dictionaries tell us, refers to stiffness or numbness, a sudden chill, a fever, especially one accompanied with fits of shivering; or rigor mortis, a stiffening of the body upon death. Although I know that many of the teacher-researchers I work with experience states similar to rigor mortis as they enter drama classrooms and engage with kids, our art form is not powered by a deadening of human emotion and subjectivity. When a recent arts philosopher argued that "all research [in drama] should be a rigorously objective quest for the truth" (Best 1996, 5), he unfortunately highlighted processes that do not sit well with an artistic-aesthetic curriculum.

While I understand the political sense of promoting the arts within a rational cognitive domain, we must not lose sight of the affective and subjective terrain in which the arts operate. Are the arts really representative of cognitive science? We must also get away from the idea that there is a truth that the arts represent. The arts don't represent a singular truth but reveal multiple truths. It would be difficult to look at a process drama, for example, in terms of one truth that was learned. There is not one truth to be learned from an arts event, but rather an experience to be had. Words like *rigorous, objective,* and *truth* are those more suited within a scientism's logic where there is an end point to be reached.

In my work with the seventh graders, for instance, we could perhaps feel that there were times when some or all of us were considerably moved or transported by the work. How do we know this to be true? What truths were the participants formulating? What is truth, anyway? Truths might emerge from a gesture, a look, a statement, a way of speaking or walking, that demonstrated a shift in understanding. Does rigor or system achieve this state? I doubt it; there was no stiffening of human process with the seventh graders, but rather a release of human thought and feeling. If participants are stirred by the work, if they feel somewhat uncomfortable, then there might be something about the quality of the experience that has released that state. In other words, it has been how that experience has been constructed and coconstructed—the transaction between the living human being and what is to be grasped, what is to be learned—that has shifted perspectives. I would want to replace a process of rigorous research with a process that:

- honors artistry
- trusts the participants' voices
- embarks on many truths
- generates a flexible and transformative approach

The qualitative dimension most comprehensively accesses the kinds of research in which I am interested, and in this respect I would like us to push the boundaries of what constitutes the rules of process drama research. There are many opponents to this view. Just as theatre audiences walked out in droves on Beckett's *Waiting for Godot* when it first premiered in London, many commentators on educational drama seem to be walking out on qualitative research.[10] "It is not mainstream," they say of the qualitative orientation, "it doesn't promote proof."

In the following claim by Bramwell (1996), which was made after she subtlely condemned the drama education community for not pursuing her "six facts" of research, she leaps into a rather peculiar justification of rigor:

> The *rigor* of the freezing of insights in experience—the drama/ theatre performance, stems from the *rigor* of drama/theatre inquiry—a freeze frame of the essence of a slice of experience embodied in imagination. (36, original emphasis)

I, for one, don't want my insights or those of my students frozen after a dramatic play encounter, nor do I think the contemplative power of theatrical performance "freezes" our reflective responses. At the heart of our response to theatre or process drama is the contemplative possibilities it arouses. The art form unsettles and disturbs. It raises and confronts consciousness. It doesn't freeze our response, it activates it, animating recurring and evocative images.

Bramwell goes on to discuss the research findings of Heathcote, Bolton, Booth, and a whole string of others as having "not proven to be worthwhile for many practitioners and so may not be said to be general and applicable research findings for that reason" (37). Perhaps we might agree with this puzzling assertion if their intention was to generate the kind of neopositivist research[11] Bramwell seeks, but even the novice drama investigator would know that Heathcote and company were not conventional researchers governed by the principles of scientism, but rather reflective practitioners who believed in the importance of critical inquiry.

I think it's unfortunate that the concerns of the mainstream empiricist, concerns governed by measurement and truth, must be seen as equally appropriate to those of the qualitative researcher. I am saddened that in our move toward the next century there are still serious misconceptions about the narrative and theatrical traditions that feed our work. I doubt that any major inroads into drama inquiry will be made until the principles of neopositivism have been convincingly debunked. Just as with *Godot* some critics failed to recognize how artistic practice operates, we must be ever watchful that those purporting to be drama researchers do not deny the qualitative spirit that powers our field. And just as I think of *Godot's* critics, who were unable to think laterally, who could value only that which had a conventional narrative structure, I am reminded of the great mainstream yearning for rational meanings, for normal rhythms, for clarity and linearity.

But I am still heartened that even within the climate in which Beckett, say, was working there were a few lone critical voices who saw something quite different in his art. "Go and see *Waiting for Godot*," wrote Hobson in London's *Sunday Times*. "At the worst you will discover a curiosity, a four-leaved clover, a black tulip; at the best something that will securely lodge in a corner of your mind for as long as you live" (quoted in Knowlson 1996, 415).

And it is in that unsettling disturbance, that sty in the eye, that we have our great justification for the arts in education. It is the four-leaved clovers, the black tulips, the disquieting discoveries that lodge in our brains that bring us to process drama. Our research must aim to get at these different curves. We must help all those studying drama education to appreciate the elasticity of the rules, the fact that the boundaries, like those in art, are constantly changing.

We are forever inventing ways to best try to recapture a happening in a drama classroom, a research method that will permit a child or a teacher to represent and to describe what they were thinking and feeling at a particular time. And in our search for invention we move beyond the mainstream design that cherishes validity and truth, beyond the neopositivist's control of the standard research techniques—beyond the obsession, in other words, for system and rigor. And it is in that journey of moving beyond system and rigor that we can best honor the life stories of the people we work with, the rich and evocative narratives that spring from and privilege the qualitative dimension in which process drama lives.

NOTES

1. Other useful works on teacher research are by Altrichter, Posch, and Somekh (1993); Cochran-Smith and Lytle (1993); Elliot (1985); Hitchcock and Hughes (1995); Kemmis (1988); Loughran and Northfield (1996); and, O'Hanlon (1996).
2. See my discussion of reflective practice in Taylor 1996, 1998.
3. I am particularly thinking of the criticism of the English theorist David Hornbrook (1989, 1991a, 1991b), who has attacked those committed to what he describes as the Newcastle school of drama. Heathcote, you might recall, worked in Newcastle-upon-Tyne. One of the problems with Hornbrook's critique is that it is motivated by a desire to have play production and theatre performance as the central activity of the drama worker; readers would note quite a different drama orientation in the practice I have outlined in this book. A further difficulty is that the criticism places little significance on the power of the learning that is possible when groups encounter process drama. The Hornbrook position seems more concerned with propositional knowledge and mainstream attainment levels.
4. Books on qualitative research by Ely (Ely et al. 1991; Ely et al. 1997), Eisner (1981, 1985, 1991), and Hitchcock and Hughes (1995) have been especially helpful to me. A good general introduction to this research design can be found in the *Handbook of Qualitative Research* (Denzin and Lincoln 1994), especially the chapter by Richardson. Other favorites include texts by Agar (1980), Burgess (1985), Goetz and LeCompte (1984), Lincoln and Guba (1985), Spradley (1979), and Van Maanen (1988). My book on research and drama education (Taylor 1996) discusses the qualitative frame of mind in more detail than I have here, and includes chapters by Cecily O'Neill, Gavin Bolton, and Margot Ely, whose work I draw on in this book.
5. Two reviews of my book *Researching Drama and Arts Education* (Taylor 1996) have been especially critical of my promotion of teacher research and the wisdom to be found from qualitative discourse (see Klein 1997; Robinson 1997). Ironically, three further

reviews (Arnold 1997; Swortzell 1997; Winston 1997) have supported the appropriateness of the qualitative mind to the dramatic art form. A colleague of mine recently suggested to me that the two negative commentaries were more an indication of the reviewers' career advancement through a quantitative research pathway. What seems more clear to me from all these reviews, both positive and negative, is how our own personal orientations and values guide how we frame and present our understandings.

6. For suggestions on how to organize log material, see Taylor (1996), especially my chapter on reflective-practitioner research. Also, most books on qualitative research include sections on how to maintain and use a logbook. Ely (1991), in particular, has extremely helpful advice on this topic.

7. See B.B.C. Omnibus (1971), Northwestern University Film Library (1973, 1974) for examples.

8. There are other archives of Heathcote's work available to the field. An impressive collection is the one held at The University of Central England, Birmingham.

9. Referring to a hand-written note of Heathcote's from 1996, Bolton (1998, 221) has shed new light on the acting behavior of the students in *Three Looms Waiting*. What looked to be "spontaneous expression of emotion" was in reality "a piece of effective contrivance" between the boy actors and the film director.

10. See Hornbrook, previously cited, and Bramwell (1996), on the importance of rigor and system in drama research.

11. Neopositivism is a concept I have explored elsewhere (Taylor, 1996). Essentially, it emerges from the quantitative researcher's desire to control output; and to measure, often numerically, human achievement.

6

The Future

If we accept that one way in which teachers can move forward in their curriculum planning is to take an active critical stance of self-inquiry, then we might concede that teachers themselves can be empowered to make some real decisions that have an impact on the quality of teaching and learning within their own classrooms. In order for teachers to make decisions, though, they need to have confidence in their own ability to influence and to effect change. One fact that seems to be ever clear to me is that teachers' work is constantly being undermined; they are frequently under fire and blamed for many of the social, economic, and educational problems of our society. Poor results in literacy, for instance, tend to be blamed on teachers' ineffectiveness; classroom management is tied into teacher competence; students' failure is related to teacher failure.

Is it any wonder that the confidence within the teaching profession is whittling away while it is under siege by folks outside the classroom who are constantly searching for scapegoats? And this lack of confidence is not only present within those teachers in schools, but also within teachers in other systems as well, such as those in universities whose performance is tied into quantifiable outputs that can be published and compared from one system to the next. Quality in educational achievements seems to be constantly sacrificed for the uniform desire for quantity; for more, not less. Given this climate it is perhaps unsurprising that many might feel that process drama and teacher research are beyond them since both demand an ability for teachers to generate rather than recycle, to produce rather than reproduce, to liberate rather than conform.

However, as I hope to remind readers in this final chapter, the future of sound pedagogical practice is geared toward teachers' and their students' believing they can exercise control over their lives. Personal freedom seems to me to be tied up in the choices we make and the choices we don't make. In my work with the seventh graders these choices were linked to three areas of my life as a seventh-grade teacher: areas related to process drama, to social studies curriculum, and to teacher research. As a consequence of my reflective practice, I was provided with some insight into each of those three areas. This insight did not occur because of any unique skill I might possess, but moreso because of a willingness to design, implement, and review a particular teaching and learning encounter. In this respect, the work described in this book is not beyond the life of any educational leader.

One feature of my work that should be clear to all is that I am not an expert possessed with special qualities, but a teacher faced with the same demands and challenges that most teachers face daily. The work in this book is governed by high points and low points, by good planning and poorly informed planning. But through my reflective practice I was able to understand more completely some features of process drama, social studies curriculum, and teacher research, and it is to that understanding that I now turn.

PRINCIPLES OF PROCESS DRAMA

Although the following principles might resonate in other subjects and disciplines, they seemed to have particular importance as I structured the process drama with my seventh graders.

Logical Order

The first principle relates to the logical sequencing of activities. In her doctoral research titled *Structure and Spontaneity: Improvisation in Theatre and Education*, O'Neill (1991c) argues that often the most significant drama experiences occur in the classroom when teachers liken themselves to "structure operators" who "weave together" the activities "in some kind of logical order" (110). This principle was later developed in her book *Drama Worlds* (1995). This weaving is not a random sequence of tasks, but a carefully planned (although not predetermined) pattern, which releases participants into a spontaneous encounter.

Throughout the Boston Massacre drama the structural arrangement of activities was partly responsible for the level of student engagement. I suspect, for example, that if we had attempted to improvise as an initial activity the Molineux meeting, it would have demanded too much from the student participants. One reason for the power of that activity was the commitment that the students had developed in their role of patriots. This commitment had been built over a number of sessions. Likewise, to have launched the process drama with a witness in the hot seat at the trial of Captain Preston might have required too much emotional energy from the group, possibly exposing the students too early to the watchful gaze of others. As O'Neill's (1995) work found, "the recurring challenge to the leader is to select *during* the process, the kind of episode or scene that will promote the development of the event to a satisfactory fulfillment" (48).

Teachers obviously have to read these matters of sequence for themselves, making their own decisions with their own students. Often, however, it seems that not enough attention and sensitivity is given in a process drama to where and how activities are positioned and generated. My own insensitivity as both the Superdupervisor and as the reluctant junior counselor indicated that even experienced drama teachers can misread the level of student engagement and miscalculate the willingness of participants to engage with the work. When such cases arise, an ability to rethink the plan and solicit student advice can also assist in the teacher's structuring. For example, the students were functioning as structure operators when they suggested why the counselor drama was unsuccessful.

The logical order that O'Neill referred to was also apparent in how the process drama was shaped. There was a reason for the focus on students' attitudes to learning coming before a focus on dramatic dilemma. The former aimed to uncover information about the students' own perceptions of when teaching and learning occurred. This information influenced my decision to ask the students to create tableaux as a beginning dramatic activity rather than asking them to improvise elaborate and lengthy scenes. To have commenced the work with the students in role as patriots having to work through a dilemma would have been, in my opinion, too demanding and logically inappropriate given the background and interests of the group. Perhaps if these seventh graders had been more experienced in drama I might not have been burdened with questions on how to protect them from unnecessary emotional exposure and personal embarrassment.

Similarly, there was a logic in having later work in the process drama address the position of the soldiers, a viewpoint that had not been heard previously, and in having the final phase focus on culminating projects. Throughout the work, therefore, there was an underlying thinking or contemplative process that influenced the decision to link and weave activities in an interrelated fashion. It would have been impossible to predetermine how the process drama would unfold or how the sequence of activities would intelligibly appear. It was, for example, only after the Molineux meeting that I believed there was a significant story of the Boston Massacre that we had overlooked. Despite the exciting work that characterized that event, I decided that we needed to probe the historical period more fully if we were to reach a comprehensive understanding of the period.

The demands of process drama require teachers to contemplate not only which activity would best fulfill an educational goal, but also where that activity could be logically placed to facilitate that goal. Many of these decisions pertaining to logical sequence are made during the course of the work.

This arrangement cannot, I believe, be generalized from one school group to the next. Process drama does not have its own intuitive logic system. The logic is socially informed and constructed based on the needs, interests, and skills of the people who experience the work. The process drama, as illustrated in this book, could not have been foreseen or predicted. It evolved, over time, constantly being redesigned, modified, and developed as it was encountered. It therefore could not be prefigured outside of the classroom context. Where and how activities are placed will depend on the contextual logic that operates in any particular group. This contextual logic is powered by a multiplicity of cultural and social factors, educational emphases and interests, which exist in each and every classroom.

Although these structural decisions on sequencing are often determined by the teacher, it is apparent that unless the student participants have an investment in them and are able to renegotiate them, then the work will not develop. For instance, I decided that to have insisted that the students improvise a scene around the liberty boys, my intended idea, would have thwarted the students' own designs, which focused on discovering more about William LeBaron. Considering the students' interest in LeBaron, it would have been illogical to impose an activity that did not accommodate their own desires. The logical structuring of activities needs to be coupled then with a sensitive pedagogic stance that empowers the teacher to read where the students are at, and then to act upon that reading.

Group Ownership

This point leads into a second principle of drama structuring, group ownership. "Drama that is done in school," wrote Teddy, "is very important because you could feel the effect + witness the experience that is happening." Teddy seems to be drawing a direct parallel here between ownership and feelings. Process drama appears particularly well placed for engaging students' feelings or emotions because it is an enactive mode of expression. Yet structuring work for group ownership so that students have a personal investment or stake in the experience is a challenging task.

If a power of the dramatic art form lies in its ability to engage students actively and communally in their own learning, then as a structural principle leaders or teachers have to consider, carefully, how and when this might happen. In my work, it was evident that the seventh graders found it a novel experience working in a variety of different groupings, often ones that would be selected by their own choices. These constantly changing groupings seemed to influence the students' sense of ownership. When Nadia observed, "Drama can take the form of teaching among ourselves," she hinted at the medium's power to expose groups to an exciting and unique form of contemplation. How, though, do these groupings promote "teaching among ourselves?" How can teachers deliberately structure for group ownership?

O'Neill's research again proves illuminating as it highlights theoretical ideas that had some bearing here. She argues that although process drama is governed by group experiences, often the most significant group moments in drama happen when the experience is shaped as a theatrical event. The leader's function in this event, she claims, "is to trap the participants in the confines of the dramatic world, as theatre workers do their audience, and then release them

into the power of co-creation as dramatists, performers and audience" (1991c, 293). Group cohesiveness and solidarity is consequently strengthened by a shared task, a challenging moment, or a
surprising discovery experienced in the process drama.

O'Neill believes that teachers might effectively entrap their students in the imaginary world when those teachers become familiar
with the great variety and breadth of skills and traditions on which
playwrights draw. Although some educators could have difficulty
with notions of entrapment, as it might suggest subversive teacher
manipulation, I find this idea a valuable concept in the structuring
of process drama.

The Molineux meeting was perhaps a more revealing example of
where the teacher-in-role as the suspicious host was deliberately
searching for a way of entrapping the students into the drama.
Tension, a fundamental element in drama, was deliberately generated in the form of the host's seeming duplicity. The patriots had
to decide how to react within those threatening and uncomfortable
circumstances. Although the students' committed responses have
been fully documented earlier, it is worth remembering the playwriting function that the students themselves exercised as they
worked as a whole group to decide on the development and future
direction of the scene. It seems clear that when opportunities are
provided for the students to construct the development of the
story, and then to take responsibility for their own playwriting decisions, they have a greater sense of investment and control in the
drama structure.

This work was characterized by "teaching among ourselves" as the
students struggled together to resolve a problem of their own design.
This session was a memorable one. Perhaps the whole group was
engaged in the work because they had to compromise ideas and
search for satisfying and realistic solutions. Such excitement in the
participants seems important in reaching group ownership.

It is difficult, however, to predict that a particular gestured or
verbalized stance in either teacher or student role-play will create
such group excitement. Part of the excitement exists because of the
spontaneity of the encounter and the challenge of improvisation.
This excitement or challenge is not unlike that experienced in a
game. The "Tory and Whig" hunt generated a quality reminiscent
of that found in the Molineux meeting: an inherent tension, group
cohesiveness, and a problem to be solved. The use of the hot seat
in later episodes also had a game element as the questioners

consciously sought to find weaknesses in the witnesses' testimony. It is useful, I believe, for teachers to examine game structure when contemplating process drama sessions, because both seem to be driven by passionate whole-group investment. Although games can also be characterized by winning and losing, a penalty system that I do not find particularly valuable in process drama, it is often how the game is played, with its varying tactics and maneuvers, that is more enthralling for the participants. In other words, the process of playing is more riveting for the group than the end result.

When Selene wrote, "Drama shouldn't be just performing little plays it could also be acting out expressions," she valued process over product, which is evident in both a game and process drama. For the group to have ownership of the work, a climate that enables participants to encounter process drama without fear of sanction appears critical. This climate, O'Neill (1991c) reminds us, must emphasize that "the experience is its own destination" (296). The leader or teacher is instrumental, I believe, in establishing an atmosphere for students to experience the structure in a process-oriented fashion. The enabling function of the leader, in this respect, is possibly the most important structural principle in process drama, and is the one to which I now turn.

The Enabling Function of the Leader

Although group ownership seems integral if students are to be committed to and involved with the work, there may be a tendency by some to forget that the teacher is a group member too. In putting too great an emphasis on student empowerment and a child-centered curriculum, there may be a diminishing understanding or recognition of the enabling function of teachers or leaders. *Enabling*, in this context, refers to the processes that "empower a person with the means to do" (Morgan and Saxton 1987, 40). Structuring process drama sessions that permit flexibility and spontaneity, that give students a voice, enabling them to believe in their own power and ability to assume leadership, is extremely complex.

This process is compounded when the cultural life of a school, as the one I was working in, with its book learning, note taking, permission slips, and disciplinary sanctions, perpetuates the attitude that the student is in a position of lower status and one who must be governed. Although the students were able to break through these barriers in their social studies classroom, this did not occur simply because the teacher decided to do process drama. Process drama, in itself, is not a liberating medium. My first encounter with the students, when I went into role as their futuristic supervisor, suggested that the teacher's narrow structuring disempowered them. It was important in that instance for me to rethink the design, without aborting it entirely, and to analyze what action steps might be implemented. This is not easy work, but when is careful and critical reflection on and in practice ever going to be easy?

However, when O'Neill (1991c) claims that "leaders in improvisation are . . . guides to new worlds, traveling with incomplete maps to the terrain, taking risks, and not knowing what lies ahead" (296), one wonders how many teachers would be prepared to accept her implied challenge. Junior high teachers, for the most part, are burdened with five hours of teaching every day, usually six hours in parochial schools. This fact is often forgotten by those who have removed themselves from the world of full-time classroom teaching. Yet despite what can be an oppressive employment reality, I believe I have revealed how crucial the teacher is in the structuring relationship. The teacher in a process drama has to structure deliberately for flexibility. He or she has to provide the opportunities for students to construct the imaginary event.

The responsibilities of teachers are therefore exceedingly arduous and ambiguous ones. Although they must provide direction, teachers have to be careful that their decisions do not constrain the needs and interests of the student participants. When negotiating whole-group dramas, such as the Molineux meeting and the junior counselors' briefing, teachers have to find ways of entrapping students without disenfranchising them. The structural framework has to allow each student to construct his or her own story within a larger one.

Teachers have to find a delicate balance between their own intentions in the drama and those of their students. In other words, they have to "lead the way," as O'Neill (1991c) aptly writes, "while walking backwards" (296). Leaders, she argues, will need "to act as guides who should know where the travelers have come from, and the nature of the journey so far, as to help to determine the kind of journey which lies ahead. In improvisation, the outcome of the journey is the journey itself" (296).

I think there has been a tendency to misjudge or undermine the importance of teachers in the educative process or journey. In championing a student-centered curriculum too loudly there may be a risk of construing the teacher's function simply as a neutral one that passively facilitates. In my classroom, I was acting in neither a neutral nor a passive mode. The teacher as enabler, therefore, holds considerable weight as a structural principle.

Within each of these principles the teacher is acting as an artist, creatively weaving the sequence into a powerful educative experience. One great challenge of process drama for teachers is that they can begin to see themselves in this way, as artists, rather than craftspersons. As I explored in Chapter 4, the craftsperson, as O'Neill (1995) writes, uses skills to achieve a predetermined end, "but the artist uses skills to discover ends through action" (64). Process drama is not governed by predetermination but by the generation of outcomes through the actual work. In this respect, teachers are always working within an artistic framework.

Although there are other structural principles pertaining to particular strategies and techniques such as teacher-in-role, small-group talk, and, in- and out-of-role reflection, it was the three principles described—sequencing of activities, group ownership, and the enabling function of the leader or teacher—that had particular prominence for this reflective practitioner.

THE DIRECTION OF SOCIAL STUDIES EDUCATION

"Drama can clarify issues and problems in social studies," wrote Albert toward the conclusion of our work on the Boston Massacre. Meryl agreed. "When you are acting out someone," she said, "you might find the similarities between you and that person." What both Albert and Meryl seemed to be alluding to was the power of drama to illuminate aspects related to historical inquiry. These illuminations, in this book, pertained not only to empathizing with Whig and Tory motivations but to more personal understandings regarding the nature of oppression, group dynamics, and how history is written and reported on.

Earlier, I described the seventh graders' perceptions of social studies. For them, social studies had been presented as a list of facts, issues and events that would need to be recalled in a chapter test. Unfortunately, the subject had been distanced so much from their own personal experiences that it was perceived as an irrelevancy, a seemingly endless battery of classes characterized by feelings of boredom and despondency. In Chapter 1 I argued that this view of the social studies is a common one among students.

If social studies teachers are concerned with energizing their curriculum so that material is presented to students in fresh and innovative ways, then my seventh graders have indicated that process drama is a method they might consider. I would hope that my attempt to engage students who had no prior experience of drama in the curriculum, might be informative to other teachers. The fact that the student participants seemed to have found the work stimulating and rewarding suggests that process drama is a powerful medium for helping students struggle with many of the contradictions that exist in the social studies.

Knowledge in the social studies, Giroux (1988) reminds us, "demands constant searching, invention and reinvention" (61). He has been critical of educators who present the social studies as valueless: "Students need to learn how to be able to move outside of their own frame of reference so that they can question the legitimacy of a given fact, concept or issue" (63). One feature of my classroom work was the manner in which students were challenged to play with historical interpretation, constantly reevaluating the worth or accuracy of a given historical view: Is William LeBaron a reliable commentator on the events of the Boston Massacre? Under what circumstances can murder be justified? Were the patriots' methods of achieving liberation fair? Can one condone self-serving behavior? How do we distinguish fact from fiction? The question of whose version can we trust in history seemed to have particular importance. How can bias and prejudice be uncovered, accounted for, and resolved?

In a process drama students often have to work through dilemmas physically, emotionally, and psychologically, so issues of the characters' motivation, commitment, reliability, and honesty are naturally at hand. Having such immediate experience in action as a reference point can richly inform the students' developing comprehension of the complexity in reconstructing a historical event. Through whose eyes is the story of history written and told? Is it important to know who is narrating the event? Can observers ever be neutral commentators? Although some educators might argue that such thinking is beyond seventh graders, my students indicated that twelve- and thirteen-year-olds are extremely capable of grappling with complex issues.

Toward the end of our work, when the witnesses were cross-examined, there was a particular example of how students can stumble into the appropriate questions when determining if someone is equivocating. I am reminded of Jessica's question to Tom during the eye-witness examination, "Are you a patriot or a loyalist?" Hearing his answer to this question would help her, she implied, form an understanding of human motivation. The question alerted her to an important issue: Political sympathies may determine a person's attitude.

One useful reason for employing process drama in the social studies classroom, then, is the immediacy and personalizing of the event, concept, or relationship being explored. This immediacy helps students experience important issues. When the students struggled in later episodes with decisions on how to narrate and construct their own version of pre-Revolutionary Boston society, they seemed to face similar problems that historians do when writing and interpreting: What events will be covered? How will those events be treated? Who will the predominant audience be, and how might this fact influence the planning? Should a deliberate interpretation of the events be included in the presentation? What means are at hand to construct the story? Process drama provides students with the opportunities to select, assemble, and analyze moments in time within a critical framework.

The seventh graders seemed to understand that a study of history cannot be divorced from the people who helped create and interpret it. "Pedagogical structures," Giroux (1988) tells us, need to be found that "promote productive communication and dialogue" (73). Productive communication, I believe, can be achieved through the immediate language contexts found in process drama. Critically examining the meaning of an eighteenth-century document or challenging the veracity of a potential witness in a trial were tasks that the seventh graders independently dealt with based on their own agendas in the structure. When Meryl wanted to discover more about why LeBaron might write negatively of the British soldiers, she was not accepting LeBaron's words at face value; she was hinting that personal biases may influence the forming of opinions.

Although Giroux does not specifically refer to process drama as a pedagogical forum,[1] I believe he would consider it an effective arena for enabling students to question and struggle with material in unique ways. Process drama is obviously not the only way in which students can appraise historical material. Yet its focus on spontaneity and improvisation fuels the encounter with much of its strength. Students not only talk about the problems they regard as significant in social studies, but they also encounter them in action.

These encounters may not always be successfully waged. Process drama is not a passive medium; it challenges students to assess, sometimes painfully, the truths surrounding the lives of individuals. When Nadia and Brenda, in role as witnesses at Preston's trial, were lambasted with a battery of questions, they had to respond carefully and quickly in ways that would satisfactorily meet the questioners' demands. To respond in a calm and composed fashion was not easy, given the implied and sometimes stated accusations of deceit that both faced. The activity highlighted how a recollection of an event can be determined by the circumstances in which it occurs. I doubt that an isolated textbook reading on historical bias or value would match the power of its immediate experience in process drama.

Although the improvised nature of process drama facilitates the kind of critical discourse and perspective that Giroux envisions in the social studies classroom, it also distinguishes it from other more traditional approaches to drama. Often when drama activities exist in social studies education they emphasize scripts, performance, and a formal audience (see Jarolimek 1990; Hennings et al. 1989; Smith 1979). However, I believe that this approach can de-emphasize what the students can bring to the material. If the characters and events of history are determined by scripted dialogue and stage directions, and if the experience of enactment is only consummated through formal production with all the accouterment of stage dressing and design, then the students are not permitted the possibility of constructing their own story or version of a historical event.

Although historical names, dates, and figures might be indelibly imprinted in the student-actors' minds as a result of such productions, the student-actors might have missed the opportunity of using the dramatic art form to raise questions and dilemmas, and play with interpretation and insight, which are central to a study of social studies.

Reconstructing a historical picture contained in a scripted play-text written by an unknown figure may be just as alienating for students as the familiar book reading and notetaking. In casting the characters, blocking the scene, and scheduling rehearsal times, the teacher perhaps reinforces the idea that drama is an elitist activity for those who can perform "well." Within this closed framework, the insights of a Molineux meeting are not permitted, nor are the evocative improvised moments of brutality LeBaron suffered, nor the chilling images of a soldier's dream. Drama is reduced to a utilitarian expediency: a neat school production with student-actors reciting memorized lines.

Process drama, however, offers the social studies teacher a method of helping students experience material in their own way with their own words, based on concerns they have generated and with which they decide to struggle. It is method that provokes the kinds of stimulations and directions in social studies education for which Giroux (1988) pleads:

> Teachers ultimately must make knowledge and experience *emancipatory* by enabling students to develop a social imagination and civic courage capable of helping them to intervene in their own self-formation, in the formation of others, and in the socially reproductive cycle of life in general. (xvii)

THE POWER OF TEACHER RESEARCH

I have intentionally used the word *power* to describe the phenomenon of teacher research. Power connotes energy, a formidable and electrifying force capable of vitalizing and transforming human behavior. Teacher research, as I wrote in the previous chapter, contains such power because the critical process of self-examination can enlighten and recharge dreary and lifeless pedagogical practices. Teacher research is the agent that can command teachers and students to explore intricately the fabric of classroom life and assess its vital elements, and it can enable them to respond to perceived strengths and weaknesses with authoritative efficacy.

Although the understanding of process drama and social studies curriculum may have bearing on the classroom practices of others, the fact that this information was gleaned from a specific classroom with a specific group at a specific time prevents them from commanding the status of general principles that would hold currency in all social studies classrooms. However, a power of teacher research lies in this precise constraint. When individual teachers are analyzing an aspect of their own teaching, and taking action following such analysis, they are inevitably in a superior position when making pedagogical decisions with their own students.

When critics of Dorothy Heathcote focus on teachers' endeavors to imitate or mimic her teaching style only to find that they (the teachers) are unable to easily replicate it, those critics highlight the flaws that occur when specific pedagogies are generalized from one classroom to the next. If such teachers were teacher-researchers, however, they perhaps would understand more about the appropriateness of a pedagogical structure as it translated in practice with their own school groups. As enchanted and mesmerized as teachers might be when they watch an effective leader at work, there is a misplaced logic operating if those teachers blindly adhere to another's approach. Whether they have stumbled upon this approach through observations or readings, teachers who are not encouraged to think for themselves in their own classrooms may not be in the best position to implement changes. I believe that the best sources of change in belief are reflection-in-action and reflection-on-action.

Perhaps it is true that the voluminous material analyzing Heathcote's teaching contrasts with the paucity of teacher researcher projects. Apparently, it is more acceptable and popular to describe the work of others than it is to describe one's own. Yet common sense dictates that reading about or observing other people's work does not mean that those observations or readings will directly influence classroom practice. Teacher research, however, anticipates that steps are taken following reflections or contemplations. In this respect, the description *teacher research* implies a critical and emancipatory form of inquiry.

One of the demands of teacher research is the intellectual pursuit that accompanies it. In my seventh-grade classroom, such pursuit could have led me in any number of directions. I could have focused on the small-group talk: How do participants negotiate in small groups? What are the responsibilities of the talkers? of the nontalkers? What decisions are required for the process drama to take shape? On the other hand, I might have focused on the students' writing in social studies: How do writing assignments interact with the process drama? When do these assignments support or weaken the work? Do the students find the assignments helpful? Both directions would have fueled my teaching with a different slant.

Furthermore, I might have started with some kind of ideological position, or a sociocultural political perspective, such as can be found in Marxist, feminist, or queer-theory literature. As it was, my focus was tied into the process drama's structure and the participants' experience of it. I was not pushing a specific ideology or theoretical position but rather I was allowing the process drama to let the students pursue the questions and issues that they were fascinated by. Different teacher researchers might have pursued various other lines of inquiry based on their own circumstances and individual readings of the work, and the extent to which they were prepared to give students ownership of the material.

The personalized nature of a given teacher research project may therefore be frustrating for readers of these reports who are intrigued with a particular issue, student, or response that has not been pursued by the leader. But it might be concluded that if the teacher-researcher did not follow a suggested path then it was not of sufficient tantalizing interest in that classroom context. For example, there was no specific focus, in this book, on how the students' responses in the process drama compared with those expressed when they were studying other topics in the social studies. My energies have been arrested here by the comprehensive analysis of one process drama. The teacher-researcher, as I stated in the previous chapter, is the principal research instrument. The researcher's assumptions, directions for inquiry, hopes, and fears are the guiding forces. It has been a central element in this book to alert readers to my own values, and particularly to the underlying assumptions that informed the classroom experience.

The intellectual pursuit of selecting focus in teacher research might be controversial given the teacher's valued reading of the lines of inquiry that should be followed in his or her own classroom. Yet this also constitutes the method's power, because teachers are making their own decisions on issues of concern to them and their students. When teachers exercise control over their own curriculum, rather than fall prey to the temptations of resource documents, textbooks, and administration dicta, they are better able to respond directly to their students. When teachers empower their own classrooms as sites of teacher research, they transcend the traditional barriers between themselves and their students, and center the educative process on a sustaining force of significant interactions.

I cannot, however, be too optimistic that teachers are able (or even willing) amid their daily routines, to assume the research stance involved in this book. It is a sobering experience listening to audiotapes, reading transcribed accounts, and watching videotapes of one's own classroom teaching. Why spend hours of time witnessing events that sometimes were poorly managed? Why consciously indulge in emotionally draining pursuits? Furthermore, at a time when educational trends are focusing more on moving power away from teachers' hands, there seems even less time for them to act upon their own reflections. If teachers are becoming *increasingly* accountable, if that is possible, to bureaucratic agencies, and if these agencies will be determining with greater pervasiveness curriculum content and its execution, why should teachers bother with teacher research?

To respond to these questions we first need to look, I believe, in our own classrooms. We need to look at students like Amara, who discovered that learning is more than reading about somebody else's ideas in a book; or like Selene, who noticed that she was able to contribute in a small group when she felt comfortable with her peers; or like Albert, who understood that his friends could richly influence his thinking; or like Tom, who celebrated his small group's filmmaking achievement. These personal student reflections signal a change in attitude, a new understanding, or an individual contentment—none of which could be, in my opinion, adequately determined by a national or statewide examination. Can teachers afford not to take a teacher research stance considering federal initiatives to determine and police national educational goals?

There is a danger that the depth and variety of individuals' educative development will be circumvented by utilitarian and functional demands. When the "Business Community" is touted as the savior who will end the heedlessness and neglect of current curricula practice, the local needs of schools are undermined. When external governmental and economic forces start dictating school practices, there seems more of an urgency for teachers to describe and document aspects of classroom life. The more teachers inquire into their classrooms, the more they may uncover about the teaching and learning process. Although teachers' discoveries may have minimal impact on the bureaucrats, they may find some way of juggling the needs of the technicians with those of their students.

Perhaps process drama might not be easily resolved within the technocrats' need for skill banks and widespread testing, but the alternative—having teachers succumb to the rhetoric that achievement correlates to statistical reporting, or that there is value in what can be measured and compared across the entire nation—

does not bode well. How do teachers score the reflections of Amara, Selene, Albert, and Tom on a national grid? How do teachers prevent themselves from submitting to the bureaucrats?

Teacher research is incompatible with succumbing. It can help magnify the capacity of teachers to think critically about practical educational concerns and therein it can possibly provide them with the strength to resist or overcome oppressive bureaucratic strategies. Ultimately it is the personal voices of Amara, Selene, Albert, Tom, and others like them that are perhaps most at risk when the distant and clinical policies of the technocrat rule. I fear the metastatic implications of training and uniform standards that drive governments, education boards, and school districts: "There is no systematic means of matching training to needs," they frequently complain, "no uniform and rigorous standards measure the skills needed and the skills learned." The lives of school children already endure a relentless and deadening battery of drills and tests.

I can only hope that the description in this book of the experience of one teacher and his students, a group of process drama workers, may empower others to take a reflection-in-action leap in their classrooms. Even though the problems of the world might not be solved in the process, at least the encounters that students and teachers have while on a satisfying adventure should invigorate, inform, and power the journey.

NOTE

1. However, Giroux's involvement with Clar Doyle's (1993) book would suggest he is committed to this method of working.

Resource List
Books on Process Drama

**MANUALS ON PROCESS DRAMA
FOR THE BEGINNER**

The books listed here have a specific commitment to the philosophy informing the drama practice in this book and have had a profound effect on the author.

Bolton, G. 1992. *New Perspectives on Classroom Drama*. Hemel Hempstead: Simon and Schuster.
Written by one of the foremost practitioners in the field, Bolton updates some of his earlier theories on classroom drama, exploring with greater clarity the nexus between artistry and practice, and includes a series of lessons for all ages.

Booth, D. 1994. *Storydrama*. Ontario: Pembroke.
A Canadian author, Booth, outlines his interest in process drama, as it relates to story and text. In Booth's process drama, stories often serve as the pretext or catalyst for group exploration; rather than being used as the script for enactment.

Booth, D., and C. Lundy. 1985. *Improvisation*. Toronto: Academic Press.
An excellent teachers' handbook that covers the variety of strategies and techniques open to the process drama worker. Numerous activities suggested.

Bunyan, P., and J. Rainer. 1996. *The Patchwork Quilt: A Cross-phase Educational Drama Project*. Sheffield: National Association for the Teaching of English.
A cross-phase educational project built around a series of encounters between an elderly woman and her past. Pitched for the top junior and early secondary years.

Burgess, R., and P. Gaudry. 1995. *Time for Drama: A Handbook for Secondary Teachers*. Milton Keynes: Longman Cheshire.
Written by Australian authors, this text provides many practical ideas for drama teachers within a sound theoretical framework. It aims to satisfy teachers' needs for drama activities but also to provide a comprehensive consideration of the dramatic process.

Fines, J., and R. Verrier. 1974. *The Drama of History*. London: New University Education.
One of the first books specifically written on the relationship between process drama and the history curriculum. The English authors examine how the work of Dorothy Heathcote might open up the world of English history.

Fleming, M. 1997. *The Art of Drama Teaching*. London: David Fulton.
This book discusses twenty-five drama techniques, each accompanied by practical examples of lessons and illustrated by an extract from a play. The author explores how dramatic form is demonstrated in playtext and process drama.

Fleming, M. 1994. *Starting Drama Teaching*. London: David Fulton.
Each chapter in this excellent introductory text contains practical ideas and examples of specific lessons from which theoretical insights into the aims and purposes of drama are derived. Current controversies are addressed, and a comprehensive guide to the published literature is provided.

Fox, M. 1987. *Teaching Drama to Young Children*. Portsmouth, NH: Heinemann.
Written for teachers of children ages five to eight who would like to teach drama but are not sure of how to begin. The author gives specific instructions on how to set up activities in which children can develop their imaginations, organizing abilities, confidence, and language.

Haseman, B., and J. O'Toole. 1986. *Dramawise: An Introduction to the Elements of Drama*. Richmond: Heinemann Educational Australia.
Activities, role-plays, and improvisations are addressed directly to the middle secondary school student. A text widely used in Australia and the U. K.

Heathcote, D., and G. Bolton. 1995. *Drama for Learning: Dorothy Heathcote's Mantle of the Expert Approach to Education*. Portsmouth, NH: Heinemann.
A thorough discussion of Heathcote's innovative mantle of the expert approach. Starting with a problem or task, teachers and students explore, in role, the knowledge they already have while making new discoveries along the way. This book is part of Heinemann's Dimensions of Drama series, edited by Cecily O'Neill.

Johnson, L., and C. O'Neill, eds. 1984. *Dorothy Heathcote: Collected Writings on Education and Drama.* London: Heinemann.
The editors have collected the most influential Heathcote papers, which cover her approach to education and learning. An important volume for those interested in probing Heathcote's praxis.

Manley, A., and C. O'Neill, eds. 1998. *Dreamseekers.* Portsmouth, NH: Heinemann.
Teachers share their process drama and African American heritage lesson plans. An important resource for those interested in multicultural issues and in ways of having students commit to the curriculum.

Marson, P., K. Brockbank, B. McGuire, and S. Morton. 1990. *Drama 14–16: A Book of Projects and Resources.* Cheltenham: Stanley Thornes.
This book offers ten thematic units with an emphasis on interaction and improvisation, but includes written assignments, discussion, and study of dramatic texts. Geared into national curriculum developments in the U. K.

Morgan, N., and J. Saxton. 1987. *Teaching Drama: A Mind of Many Wonders.* London: Hutchinson.
A comprehensive and popular handbook for all drama teachers written in an accessible style. Each chapter focuses on one skill—its advantages, how to use it, problems and solutions, tried-and-tested examples and skill-building exercises for the teacher to consolidate the learning.

Neelands, J. 1990. *Structuring Drama Work: A Handbook of Available Forms in Theatre and Drama,* edited by Tony Goode. Cambridge, England: Cambridge University Press.
A practical handbook for drama teachers and youth theatre workers. It offers a range of theatrical conventions to help initiate, focus, and develop dramatic activity.

O'Neill, C., and A. Lambert. 1982. *Drama Structures: A Practical Handbook for Beginners.* London: Hutchinson.
One of the most influential texts on how process drama is experienced by students. Each of the lessons documented has been taught with students, and the authors demonstrate the kind of choices open to teachers given the responses of the group.

O'Neill, C., A. Lambert, R. Linnell, and J. Warr-Wood. 1976. *Drama Guidelines.* London: Heinemann.
An earlier shorter version of Drama Structures. *A most accessible introduction to the key principles that inform process drama. A nonthreatening collection of activities are proposed for the beginning teacher with an emphasis on the "learning through" possibilities that are generated from process drama.*

O'Toole, J. 1992. *The Process of Drama: Negotiating Art and Meaning.* London: Routledge.
Explores the relationships between the playwright, the elements of dramatic art, and the other artists involved in the process of drama. Areas covered include: the dramatic context; roles and relationships; the drama space; language, movement and gesture; tension and the audience.

Readman, G., and G. Lamont. 1994. *Drama.* London: BBC Educational Publishing.
Written primarily for the British nonspecialist primary teacher, there are numerous suggestions for planning, implementation, and assessment as well as how drama might facilitate national educational priorities.

Swartz, L. 1995. *Dramathemes.* Portsmouth, NH: Heinemann.
Written by a popular Canadian elementary school teacher, this text is an excellent introduction to drama in the classroom, and provides a structured thematic approach towards lesson planning and implementation. Teachers love this book.

Tarlington, C., and P. Verriour. 1983. *Offstage: Elementary Education Through Drama.* Toronto: Oxford University Press.
This book addresses itself to the generalist elementary teacher, providing suggestions for integration into other areas of the curriculum, especially language arts and social studies.

Taylor, P., ed. 1995. *Pre-text and Storydrama: The Artistry of Cecily O'Neill and David Booth.* Brisbane: National Association for Drama in Education. (Available from the NADIE Office, Australia, c/o NADIE Administrator, Metro Arts, 109 Edward Street, Brisbane QLD 4000 Australia)
A short monograph that examines two key aspects of process drama, which have been developed by the field's leaders, pre-text and storydrama. The monograph follows the practice of O'Neill and Booth and includes the responses of teachers and the students to process drama.

Wooland, B. 1993. *The Teaching of Drama in the Primary School.* London: Longman.
An excellent book that introduces process drama to the elementary school teacher. While informed by policies developed in British national curriculum and how process drama might achieve key attainment levels, the book will be accessible to teachers elsewhere.

FOR THOSE MORE
THEORETICALLY MINDED

Bolton, G. 1984. *Drama in Education*. London: Longman.
Bolton takes the reader through some of the major historical emphases on the development of process drama and makes a compelling case as to why drama should be at the center of the curriculum.

Bolton, G. 1979. *Towards a Theory of Drama in Education*. London: Longman.
One of the first theoretical works on how process drama is different from other modes of drama activity in schools. Bolton proposes four types of drama and then outlines why type four (drama for learning) is a powerful educative tool.

Booth, D. 1987. *Drama Words: The Role of Drama in Language Growth*. Toronto: Language Study Centre, Toronto Board of Education.
An important study on the relationship between drama and language. Booth explores how the intentions of the language teacher can be supported by the process drama worker. This book is an excellent resource for language teachers interested in using drama in the classroom.

Byron, K. 1986. *Drama in the English Curriculum*. New York: Methuen.
A cleverly constructed text, written as a series of journal entries between a beginning teacher and a more experienced one. The focus is on how drama can be introduced into the language arts curriculum. Numerous examples of using drama to explore text are provided. An excellent resource for the language literacy teacher interested in using drama but unsure how to begin.

Davis, D., and C. Lawrence. 1986. *Gavin Bolton: Selected Writings*. London: Longman.
A comprehensive selection of twenty-six of the best and most useful of Gavin Bolton's papers, articles, and essays. Subjects covered include the nature of children's drama, drama and emotion, implications for drama as an artform, and drama and teaching/learning.

Heathcote, D. 1980. *Drama as Context*. Aberdeen: National Association for the Teaching of English.
Part One describes the Ozymandias Saga, a project on the theme of conquest, which was undertaken with children in a Newcastle (U. K.) primary school. Part Two describes an experiment in teacher education in which Heathcote demonstrated an approach to text that was designed to deepen understanding of Brecht's play Caucasian Chalk Circle *and the role of the teacher in the classroom.*

McLean, J. 1996. *An Aesthetic Framework in Drama: Issues and Implications*. Brisbane: NADIE Publications. (Available from the NADIE

Administrator, Metro Arts Building, 109 Edward Street, Brisbane 4000 Australia)
This research monograph, the second paper in the NADIE Research Monograph Series, demystifies the aesthetic and encourages teachers to develop their own aesthetic consciousness in order to place the aesthetic confidently at the center of their drama teaching.

Muir, A. 1996. *New Beginnings: Knowledge and Form in the Drama of Bertolt Brecht and Dorothy Heathcote.* Stoke-on-Trent: Trentham Books.
This monograph forms part of a series of works on education from the University of Central England. Muir focuses on Brecht and Heathcote, contrasting their understanding of human understanding and dramatic form.

O'Neill, C. 1995. *Drama Worlds: A Framework for Process Drama.* Portsmouth, NH: Heinemann.
This book considers process drama's sources and its connections with more familiar kinds of improvisation: the text it generates, the kinds of roles available, its relation to the audience and dramatic time, and the leader's function in the event. Many examples of process dramas provided. This is the first book in Heinemann's Dimensions of Drama series, edited by Cecily O'Neill.

Peter, M. 1995. *Making Drama Special: Developing Drama Practice to Meet Special Educational Needs.* London: David Fulton.
The author has written a practical guide for developing reflective drama practice in relation to pupils with learning difficulties, taking account of the particular pressures presented by such challenging teaching situations.

Taylor, P., ed. 1996. *Researching Drama and Arts Education: Paradigms and Possibilities.* London: Falmer Press.
A handbook that covers the various research methods available to the field, including action research, reflective practice, historical inquiry, and quasi-experimental.

Wagner, B. J. 1976. *Dorothy Heathcote: Drama as a Learning Medium.* Washington, DC: National Education Association.
Given that Heathcote has never written a book by herself, Wagner's documentation of her evolving practice in the early 1970s is an important contribution to the field. While Heathcote's ideas shifted markedly from the time when this book was first published, the power of her work is clearly apparent and some of the key principles that informed her early practice are outlined.

Bibliography

Abbs, P. 1994. *The Educational Imperative*. London: Falmer Press.

Agar, M. 1980. *The Professional Stranger*. Orlando, FL: Academic Press.

Allen, J. 1979. *Drama in Schools: Its Theory and Practice*. London: Heinemann.

Altrichter, H., P. Posch, and B. Somekh. 1993. *Teachers Investigate Their Work: An Introduction to the Methods of Action Research*. London: Routledge.

Arnold, R. 1997. Book review. *NADIE Journal* 20 (1): 97–100.

Atwell, N. 1987. *In the Middle*. Portsmouth, NH: Heinemann.

Barton, B., and D. Booth. 1990. *Stories in the Classroom*. Portsmouth, NH: Heinemann.

B.B.C. Omnibus. 1971. *Three Looms Waiting*. Film. London: B.B.C. 52 minutes.

Beckerman, B. 1970. *Dynamics of Drama*. New York: Knopf.

Berthoff, A. 1981. *The Making of Meaning: Metaphors, Models, and Maxims for Writing*. Montclair, NJ: Boynton/Cook.

Best, D. 1996. "Understanding Artistic Experience: Some Vital Pointers for Research." *NADIE Journal* 20(2): 41–52.

Bissex, G., and R. Bullock, eds. 1987. *Seeing for Ourselves*. Portsmouth, NH: Heinemann.

Boal, A. 1985. *Theatre of the Oppressed*. New York: Theatre Communications Group.

Bolton, G. 1998. *Acting in Classroom Drama: A Critical Analysis*. Stoke on Trent, England: Trentham Books.

———. 1992. *New Perspectives on Classroom Drama*. Hempel Hempstead: Simon and Schuster.

———. 1986. *Selected Writings*. New York: Longman.

———. 1985a. "Gavin Bolton interviewed by David Davis." *2D* 4 (2): 4–14.

———. 1985b. "Changes in Thinking About Drama in Education." *Theory into Practice* XXIV (3): 151–57.

———. 1984. *Drama as Education*. Essex: Longman.

———. 1979. *Towards a Theory of Drama in Education*. London: Longman.

BOOTH, D. 1994. *Storydrama*. Ontario: Pembroke.

———. 1987. *Drama Words*. Toronto: Language Study Center.

———. 1986. *Games for Everyone*. Ontario: Pembroke.

———. 1985. "Imaginary Gardens with Real Toads." *Theory into Practice* 24 (3): 193–98.

BRAMWELL, R. 1996. "Resisting Shadows Which Combat Cooperation." *DRAMA—The Journal of National Drama* 4 (3): 34–37.

BRUNER, J. 1986. *Actual Minds, Possible Worlds*. Cambridge, MA: Harvard University Press.

———. 1966. *Towards a Theory of Instruction*. Cambridge, MA: Harvard University Press.

———. 1962. *On Knowing*. Cambridge, MA: Belknap.

BRUNNER, D. D. 1994. *Inquiry and Reflection: Framing Narrative Practice in Education*. Albany: State University of New York Press.

BURGESS, R., ed. 1985. *Field Methods in the Study of Education*. London: Falmer Press.

BURGESS, R., and P. GAUDRY. 1985. *Time for Drama*. Milton Keynes, England: Open University.

BYRON, K. 1986. *Drama in the English Classroom*. New York: Methuen.

CALKINS, L. 1985. *Lessons from a Child*. Portsmouth, NH: Heinemann.

———. 1982. *Lessons from a Child: A Case Study of One Child's Growth in Writing*. Unpublished doctoral dissertation, New York University.

CARPENTER, H. M. 1969 "The Role of Skills in Elementary Social Studies." In *Readings for Social Studies in Elementary Education*, edited by J. Jarolimek and H. M. Walsh, 151–57. Toronto: Macmillan.

CARR, W., and S. KEMMIS. 1986. *Becoming Critical: Knowing Through Action Research*. 2d ed. Barcombe: Falmer Press.

CARROLL, J. 1996. "Escaping the Information Abattoir: Critical and Transformative Research in Drama Classrooms." In *Researching*

Drama and Arts Classrooms: Paradigms and Possibilities, edited by P. Taylor, 72–84. London: Falmer.

CLARKE, M. A. 1989. "Negotiating Agendas: Preliminary Considerations." *Language Arts Journal* 66 (4): 371–79.

CLEGG, D. 1973. "The Dilemma of Drama in Education." *Theatre Quarterly* 3: 9.

COCHRAN-SMITH, M., and S. LYTLE. 1993. *Inside/Outside: Teacher Research and Knowledge.* New York: Teachers College Press.

CONSORTIUM OF NATIONAL ARTS EDUCATION ASSOCIATIONS. 1994. *National Standards for Arts Education: What Every Young American Should Know and Be Able to Do in the Arts.* Reston, VA: Music Educators National Conference.

COOK, C. 1917. *The Play Way.* New York: Frederick A. Stokes.

COURTNEY, R. 1997. *The Quest: Research and Inquiry in Arts Education.* 2d ed. Lanham, MD: University Press of America.

DENZIN, N., and Y. LINCOLN, eds. 1994. *Handbook of Qualitative Research.* Thousand Oaks, CA: Sage.

DEWEY, J. [1938] 1963. *Experience and Education.* New York: Macmillan.

———. [1934] 1958. *Art as Experience.* New York: Minton, Balch and Company.

———. [1933] 1991. *How We Think.* Boston: Heath.

———. [1916] 1944. *Democracy and Education.* New York: Macmillan.

———. [1915] 1921. *The School and Society.* Chicago: University of Chicago Press.

DONALDSON, M. 1978. *Children's Minds.* London: Tavistock.

DOYLE, C. 1993. *Raising Curtains on Education: Drama as a Site for Critical Pedagogy.* Westport, CT: Bergin and Garvey.

DUCKWORTH, E. 1987. *"The Having of Wonderful Ideas" and Other Essays on Teaching and Learning.* New York: Teachers College Press.

EISNER, E. 1991. *The Enlightened Eye: Qualitative Inquiry and the Enchantment of Educational Practice.* New York: Macmillan.

———. 1985. *The Art of Educational Evaluation.* London: Falmer Press.

———. 1981. "The Role of the Arts in Cognition and Curriculum." *Phi Delta Kappan* 63 (1): 48–52.

ELLIOT, J. 1985. "Facilitating Action Research in Schools: Some Dilemmas." In *Field Methods in the Study of Education,* edited by R. Burgess. London: Falmer Press.

ELLIOT, J., and C. ADELMAN. 1976. *Innovation at the Classroom Level: A Case Study of the Ford Teaching Project.* Milton Keynes: Open University.

ELY, M., R. VINZ, M. DOWNING, and M. ANZUL. 1997. *On Writing Qualitative Research: Living by Words.* London: Falmer Press.

ELY, M., M. ANZUL, T. FRIEDMAN, D. GARNER, and A. M. STEINMETZ. 1991. *Doing Qualitative Research: Circles Within Circles.* New York: Falmer Press.

ERIKSSON, S. 1995. "The Violence Workshop." *NJ* 19 (1): 65–77.

FAULKES-JENDYK, M. 1975. "Creative Dramatic Leaders Face Objective Examination." *Canadian Child and Youth Drama Association Bulletin.*

FLEMING, M. 1997. *The Art of Drama Teaching.* London: David Fulton.

FINES, J., and R. VERRIER. 1974. *The Drama of History.* London: New University Education.

FITZGIBBON, E. 1997. "Crossing the Boundaries: Drama as Subject and Method." *Drama Matters* 2 (1): 5–18.

FREIRE, P. 1970. *Pedagogy of the Oppressed.* New York: Continuum.

FYFE, H. 1996. "Drama in the Context of a Divided Society." In *Drama, Culture, and Empowerment: The IDEA Dialogues,* edited by J. O'Toole and K. Donelan. Brisbane: IDEA Publications.

GARDNER, D. 1965. "Emotions: A Basis for Learning." In *Feelings and Learning.* Washington, DC: Association for Childhood Education International.

GIROUX, H. 1988. *Teachers as Intellectuals.* Granby, MA: Bergin & Garvey.

GOETZ, J., and M. LECOMPTE. 1984. *Ethnography and Qualitative Design in Educational Research.* Orlando, FL: Academic Press.

GOSWAMI, D., and P. STILLMAN, eds. 1987. *Reclaiming the Classroom: Teacher Research as an Agency for Change.* Portsmouth, NH: Boynton/Cook.

GREENE, M. 1995. *Releasing the Imagination: Essays on Education, the Arts, and Social Change.* San Francisco: Jossey-Bass.

GRUNDY, S. 1987. *Curriculum: Product or Praxis.* London: Falmer Press.

HANNA, P. R. 1987. *Assuring Quality for the Social Studies in Our Schools.* Stanford, CA: Hoover Institution.

HEATHCOTE, H. 1990. Keynote address. In *The Fight for Drama: The Fight for Education,* edited by K. Byron. Newcastle Upon Tyne: NATD Printers Inc.

————. 1984a. "Dorothy Heathcote's Notes." In *Dorothy Heathcote: Collected Writings on Education and Drama,* edited by L. Johnson and C. O'Neill, 202–10. London: Hutchinson.

————. 1984b. "Signs and Portents." In *Dorothy Heathcote: Collected Writings on Education and Drama,* edited by L. Johnson and C. O'Neill, 160–70. London: Hutchinson.

————. 1984c. "Drama as a Process for Change." In *Dorothy Heathcote: Collected Writings on Education and Drama,* edited by L. Johnson and C. O'Neill, 114–25. London: Hutchinson.

————. 1984d. "Improvisation." In *Dorothy Heathcote: Collected Writings on Education and Drama,* edited by L. Johnson and C. O'Neill, 44–48. London: Hutchinson.

————. 1981. "Drama as Education." In *Children and Drama,* edited by N. McCaslin, 78–90. New York: Longman.

————. 1980. "From the Particular to the Universal." In *Exploring Theatre and Education,* edited by K. Robinson, 7–50. London: Heinemann.

————. 1971. "Subject or System?" In *Drama and Theatre in Education,* edited by N. Dodd and W. Hickson, 42–62. London: Heinemann.

HEATHCOTE, D., and G. BOLTON. 1995. *Drama for Learning: Dorothy Heathcote's Mantle of the Expert Approach to Education.* Portsmouth, NH: Heinemann.

HEIKKINEN, H. 1997. "Shaken, Not Stirred." *Research in Drama Education* 2 (1): 114–17.

HENNINGS, D. G., G. HENNINGS, and S. F. BANICH. 1989. *Today's Elementary Social Studies.* New York: Harper and Row.

HILLMAN, J. 1983. *Healing Fiction.* Barrytown, NY: Station Hill.

HIRSCH, E. D. 1987. *Cultural Literacy.* Boston: Houghton Mifflin.

HITCHCOCK, G., and D. HUGHES. 1995. *Research and the Teacher: A Qualitative Introduction to School-based Research.* 2d ed. London: Routledge.

HODGSON, J., and E. RICHARDS. 1966. *Improvisation.* London: Methuen.

HOPKINS, D. 1985. *A Teacher's Guide to Classroom Research.* Milton Keynes: Open University.

HORNBROOK, D. 1991a. *Education in Drama.* London: Falmer Press.

————. 1991b. "Can We Do Ours, Miss? Towards a Dramatic Curriculum." *The Drama/Theatre Teacher* 4 (2): 15–19.

————. 1989. *Education and Dramatic Art.* Oxford: Blackwell.

HUGHES, J., ed. 1991. *Drama in Education: The State of the Art.* NSW, Australia: Educational Drama Association.

JAROLIMEK, J. 1990. *Social Studies in Elementary Education.* New York: Macmillan.

JAROLIMEK, J. 1977. *Social Studies Competencies and Skills.* New York: Macmillan.

JOHNSON, L., and C. O'NEILL, eds. 1984. *Dorothy Heathcote: Collected Writings on Drama in Education.* London: Hutchinson.

KEMMIS, S. 1988. "Action Research in Retrospect and Prospect." In *The Action Research Reader,* 3d ed., edited by S. Kemmis and R. McTaggart, 27–40. Geelong, Australia: Deakin University.

KEMMIS, S., and R. MCTAGGART. 1988. *The Action Research Planner.* 3d ed. Victoria: Deakin University.

KIDDER, F. 1870. *History of the Boston Massacre.* Albany, NY: Munsell.

KIRBY, M. 1965. *Happenings.* New York: Dutton.

KINCHELOE, J. 1991. *Teachers as Researchers: Qualitative Inquiry as a Path to Empowerment.* London: Falmer Press.

KLEIN, J. 1997. "Books in Review." *STAGE of the Art* 9 (2): 27–30.

KNOWLSON, J. 1996. *The Life of Samuel Beckett.* London: Bloomsbury.

LANGER, S. 1953. *Feeling and Form.* New York: Charles Scribner's Sons.

LEWIN, K. 1946. "Action Research and Minority Problems." *Journal of Social Issues* 2: 34–46.

LINCOLN, Y., and E. GUBA. 1985. *Naturalistic Inquiry.* Beverly Hills, CA: Sage.

LOUGHRAN, J., and J. NORTHFIELD. 1996. *Opening the Classroom Door: Teacher, Researcher, Learner.* London: Falmer Press.

MARTIN, N. 1987. "On the Move." In *Reclaiming the Classroom,* edited by S. Goswami and P. Stillman, 20–27. Portsmouth, NH: Heinemann.

MCLAREN, P. 1989. *Life in Schools.* New York: Longman.

MCLAREN, P., and J. GIARELLI, eds. 1995. *Critical Theory and Educational Research.* Albany: State University of New York Press.

MCKERNAN, J. 1996. *Curriculum Action Research: A Handbook of Methods and Resources for the Reflective Practitioner.* 2d ed. London: Kogan Page.

MCLEAN, J. 1996. *An Aesthetic Framework in Drama.* Brisbane: NADIE Publications.

Morgan, N., and J. Saxton. 1996. "And a River Runs Through It." In *Drama, Culture, and Empowerment: The IDEA Dialogues,* edited by J. O'Toole and K. Donelan, 233–40. Brisbane: IDEA Publications.

————. 1987. *Teaching Drama.* London: Hutchinson.

Muir, A. 1996. *New Beginnings: Knowledge and Form in the Drama of Bertolt Brecht and Dorothy Heathcote.* Stoke-on-Trent: Trentham Books.

National Council for the Social Studies Task Force on Scope and Sequence. 1989. "In Search of a Scope and Sequence." *Social Education* (October): 376–87.

Neelands, J. 1990. *Structuring Drama Work.* Cambridge, England: Cambridge University Press.

Newmann, F. M. 1988. "Higher-Order Thinking in High School Studies." Report by National Center on Effective Secondary Schools. Madison: University of Wisconsin.

Northwestern University Film Library. 1974. *Building Belief, Parts I and II.* Film. Evanston, Illinois: Northwestern University. 28 minutes and 29 minutes.

————. 1973. *Dorothy Heathcote Talks to Teachers, Parts I and II.* Film. Illinois: Northwestern University. 30 minutes and 32 minutes.

O'Hanlon, C., ed. 1996. *Professional Development Through Action Research in Educational Settings.* London: Falmer Press.

O'Neill, C. 1995. *Drama Worlds: A Framework for Process Drama.* Portsmouth, NH: Heinemann.

————. 1991a. "Dramatic Worlds: Structuring for Significant Experience." *The Drama/Theatre Teacher* 4 (1): 3–5.

————. 1991b. "Drama in the Classroom: The Search for Dramatic Action." In *Drama in Education: The State of the Art,* edited by J. Hughes, 33–43. Sydney, Australia: Educational Drama Association.

————. 1991c. Structure and Spontaneity: Improvisation in Theatre and Education. Unpublished doctoral dissertation, University of Exeter.

————. 1989a. "Empathy and Interpretation: Drama Activities in the English Classroom." In *On-Site Proceedings: International Drama Education Research Symposium,* edited by J. Wilkinson, 1–16. Winnipeg, MB: Canadian Child and Youth Drama Press.

————. 1989b. "Dialogue and Drama: The Transformation of Events, Ideas and Teachers." *Language Arts* 66 (5): 528–40.

————. 1988. "Ways of Seeing: Audience Function in Drama and Theatre." *The NADIE Journal* 13 (1): 11–17.

————. 1985. "Imagined Worlds in Theatre and Drama." *Theory into Practice* 24: 158–65.

————. 1983. "Role Play and Text." *The English Magazine* 11.

————. 1978. Drama and the Web of Form: An Attempt to Isolate the Elements of Aesthetic Form and Their Operation Within the Process of Educational Drama. Unpublished master's thesis, University of Durham.

O'NEILL, C., and A. LAMBERT. 1982. *Drama Structures*. London: Hutchinson.

O'TOOLE, J., and K. DONELAN, eds. 1996. *Drama, Culture, and Empowerment: The IDEA Dialogues*. Brisbane, Australia: IDEA Publications.

PARKER, W. C. 1991. *Renewing the Social Studies Curriculum*. Alexandria, VA: Association for Supervision and Curriculum Development.

PHELAN, M. K. 1976. *The Story of the Boston Massacre*. New York: Thomas Crowell.

RASMUSSEN, B. 1996. "Another Apologetic Reappearance." In *Drama, Culture, and Empowerment: The IDEA Dialogues,* edited by J. O'Toole and K. Donelan, 131–39. Brisbane, Australia: IDEA Publications.

RICHARDSON, L. 1994. "Writing: A Method of Inquiry." In *Handbook of Qualitative Research,* edited by N. Denzin and Y. Lincoln. Thousand Oaks, CA: Sage.

ROBINSON, K. 1997. Book review. *Research in Drama Education* 2 (1): 126–28.

SANDELOWSKI, M. 1993. "Rigor or Rigor Mortis: The Problem of Rigor in Qualitative Research Revisited." *Advances in Nursing Science* 162: 1–8.

SCHEFF, T. 1979. *Catharsis in Healing, Ritual, and Drama*. Los Angeles: University of California Press.

SCHÖN, D. 1992. "The Theory of Inquiry: Dewey's Legacy to Education." *Curriculum Inquiry* 22 (2): 119–39.

————. 1983. *The Reflective Practitioner*. New York: Basic Books.

SMITH, J. A. 1979. *Creative Teaching of the Social Studies in the Elementary School*. Boston: Allyn and Bacon.

SOBEL, R., R. LaRaus, L. A. DE LEON, and H. P. MORRIS. 1982. *The Challenge of Freedom*. River Forest, IL: Laidlaw.

SOMERS, J., ed. 1996. *Drama and Theatre in Education: Contemporary Research*. North York, Ontario: Captus Press.

SPRADLEY, J. P. 1979. *The Ethnographic Interview*. New York: Holt, Rinehart and Winston.

THE STATE EDUCATION DEPARTMENT. 1987. *Social Studies 7–8: United States and New York State History.* Albany, NY: State Education Department.

STENHOUSE, L. 1975. *Introduction to Curriculum Research and Development.* London: Heinemann.

SWORTZELL, N. 1997. Book review. *Drama Matters* 2 (1): 81–85.

TARLINGTON, C., and P. VERRIOUR. 1991. *Role Drama.* Ontario: Pembroke Press.

TAYLOR, P. 1998. "Reflective Practitioner Research." In *Educational Drama and Language Arts: What Research Shows,* edited by B. J. Wagner, 212–30. Portsmouth, NH: Heinemann.

———. 1997. "Australian Research." *Australian Drama Education Magazine* 3: 10–17.

———, ed. 1996. *Researching Drama and Arts Education: Paradigms and Possibilities.* London: Falmer Press.

———. 1995a. "Our Adventure of Experiencing: Reflective Practice and Drama Research. *Youth Theatre Journal* 9: 31–52.

———. 1995b. *Pre-text and Storydrama: The Artistry of Cecily O'Neill and David Booth.* NADIE Research Monograph Series, Brisbane, Australia: NADIE Publications.

———. 1992. Our Adventure of Experiencing: Drama Structure and Action Research in a Grade Seven Social Studies Classroom. Doctoral dissertation, *University Microfilms International,* Ann Arbor, MI, No. 9237780.

———. 1991a. "Playing with Form: Part Two." *The NADIE Journal* 15 (3): 3–12.

———. 1991b. "Editorial on Structuring Drama Sessions." *The Drama/Theatre Teacher* 4 (1): 2.

———. 1990a. "A Raisin in the Sun: A Drama Education Workshop." *MASK* 13 (2): 18–21.

———. 1990b. "Thoughts on Narrative, Positivism, and Ethnography." *The NADIE Journal* 14 (2): 2–5.

———. 1989. "Drama and Literacy: A Reappraisal." *The NADIE Journal* 13 (2): 44–49.

VAN MAANEN, J. 1988. *Tales of the Field: On Writing Ethnography.* Chicago: University of Chicago Press.

VERHOVEK, S. H. 1991. "Plan to Emphasize Minority Cultures Ignites a Debate." *The New York Times,* 21 June, B4.

VERRIOUR, P. 1989. "Bolton and *The Crucible* Drama." *NADIE Journal* 13 (2): 12–15.

VYGOTSKY, L. S. 1978. *Mind in Society: The Development of Higher Psychological Processes.* Cambridge, MA: Harvard University Press.

WAGNER, B. J. 1998. *Educational Drama and Language Arts.* Portsmouth, NH: Heinemann.

———. 1988. "Does Classroom Drama Affect the Arts of Language? *Language Arts* 65 (1).

———. 1986. The Effects of Role Playing on Written Persuasion: An Age and Channel Comparison of Fourth and Eighth Graders. Dissertation, University of Illinois at Chicago. UMI 8705196.

———. 1976. *Dorothy Heathcote: Drama as a Learning Medium.* Washington, DC: National Education Association.

WARD, W. 1957. *Playmaking for Children.* New York: Appleton-Century-Crofts.

———. 1952. *Stories to Dramatize.* Anchorage: Anchorage Press.

———. 1930. *Creative Dramatics* New York: Appleton.

WAY, B. 1967. *Development Through Drama.* London: Longman.

WELLS, G. 1986. *The Meaning Makers: Children Learning Language and Using Language to Learn.* Portsmouth, NH: Heinemann.

WHITE, H. 1987. *The Content of the Form: Narrative Discourse and Historical Representation.* Baltimore, MD: Johns Hopkins University Press.

WINSTON, J. 1997. Book review. *Research in Drama Education* 2 (1): 123–26.

ZOBEL, H. B. 1970. *The Boston Massacre.* New York: Norton.